FREESTYLE

ILLUSTRATING URBAN FASHION

GINGKO PRESS

I0112794

FREESTYLE

ILLUSTRATING URBAN FASHION

ISBN 978-1-58423-670-2

First Published in the United States of America by
Gingko Press by arrangement with
Sandu Publishing Co., Ltd.

Gingko Press, Inc.
1321 Fifth Street
Berkeley, CA 94710 USA
Tel: (510) 898 1195
Fax: (510) 898 1196
Email: books@gingkopress.com
www.gingkopress.com

SANDU ☰ | 360

Copyright © 2017 by Sandu Publishing
First published in 2017 by Sandu Publishing

Sponsored by Design 360°
– Concept and Design Magazine

Edited and produced by
Sandu Publishing Co., Ltd.

Book design, concepts & art direction by
Sandu Publishing Co., Ltd.
Chief Editor: Wang Shaoqiang
Design Director: Niu Huizhen

Illustration on front cover, title page,
and page 003 by Mr Woody Woods.
Illustration on page 004-007
and page 233-240 by Valístika Studio.

info@sandupublishing.com
www.sandupublishing.com

All rights reserved. No part of this publication may
be reproduced or transmitted in any form or by
any means, electronic or mechanical, including
photocopy, recording or any information storage and
retrieval system, without prior permission in writing
from the publisher.

Printed and bound in China

CONTENTS

PREFACE

•By Valístika Studio

Urban fashion has had a strong relationship with illustration from the beginning. The first streetwear companies drew references freely from sources including rock album covers, skate T-shirts and graffiti writing to create its gestural style. The form exploded in late 1980s and early 1990s as urban fashion made its mark on the graphic textile world, steeped in sarcasm and humor during this rebellious period, when punk's noise was fading and hip-hop's boom was on the rise.

In this whirlwind of creativity and freedom the first cool brands emerged in the United States. Backed by graffiti artists, skateboarding legends, and personalities from the punk-rock and hip-hop movements, designs from Santa Cruz, Fuct, Stussy and many others began to take off. These urban brands meet the definition of "fashion", but unlike ready-to-wear or haute couture firms, these creators looked for references that others might not appreciate. Through collaborations with artists, these leading brands shared with their audience a love of illustration portrayed in a more independent and communicative way. Back then, small brands took their creations in a more independent and underground direction, focusing on their inner-circles and on one target — "If you met someone wearing the same brand as you, it was cool and there was a connection." These brands acted as a direct reference to "that present" and offered a reflection of the current social trends.

It is often said "do not judge a book by its cover," which is usually a good rule of thumb, but in the world of textile graphics, the "cover" is the "key." The first "visual hit" is the one that rules a design — the color palette, graphic style, and attention to details are what will make a piece of work a winning design. Sometimes garments do not even need to be good, they are simply sold on the basis of a promoter's reputation or thanks to the fame of a brand. But that is not what we are talking about, we are talking about quality, fine-work, experience, and correct color choices on garments. Over the years, the technical possibilities for reproducing graphics on garments have gone from a couple of stamping techniques, to the opening up of a huge range of unbelievable printing effects. Still, for us designers, ideas have to prevail to achieve a winning design — the more direct and powerful the graphic, the greater its impact on the public. We are convinced that a person is identified by the garments that he or she is wearing based on the overall graphic style. If a designer strikes the right chord, people will want that piece of clothing above all others.

Having the opportunity to create specific urban fashion collections is a real pleasure. We have always been very interested in this world, so we have immersed ourselves in it, but without leaving aside other possible graphic applications. When we are working on graphics, the challenge is to make every effort to try to raise that product to a "HYPE" category. In other words, our objective is for people to like the design so much that it runs out quickly. Under this model we will have more opportunities to keep on doing what we love.

"If you put your heart into something, the public will notice and value it." And if it is something that few can have, the inner voice speaks louder. In our opinion, we must forget conventions and flat shirts, take risks, have fun making graphics and designing original and impactful garments cut from good fabrics.

It seems that in recent years, because of the economic crisis and recession, conformity has taken root, with sales and marketing prevailing over risk-taking and innovation. However, the call for creativity and originality still exists as some larger companies have initiated interesting collaborations in the form of "Limited Editions" with graffiti artists, illustrators, and leading designers from all over the world. Perhaps more importantly, there are still many independent brands acting on principle and passion in the pursuit of iconic graphic-driven garment design.

For this newest urban generation, knowledge of the past will inform its future! In *Freestyle — Illustrating Urban Fashion*, you will see many great artists setting their sights on exploring the present urban era, which will surely become the inspiration of the next generation.

Valístika Studio

Formed in 2006, Valístika is a visual studio based in Madrid, focusing on illustration, typography, branding, and graphics applied to clothing, advertising, editorial, and all fields related to print and motion media. They work with clients all over the globe.

www.valistika.com

CAPSULES & COLLECTIONS

Valístika Studio

Formed in 2006, Valístika is a visual studio focusing on illustration, typography, branding, and graphics applied to clothing, advertising, editorial, and all fields related to print and motion media.

INTERVIEW

– What originally drove you to establish Valístika? Please tell us more about your studio.

Valístika is simply two people working in one direction, Guadalupe and Miguel. We met in 2001 when studying in Madrid and we never separated from each other again. In 2006 we set up Valístika and moved to various cities, but finally we came back to Madrid. "Valístika" is a term modified from "balística" which in English means "ballistic" and refers to the motion of objects moving under their own momentum and the force of gravity. We love the sound and the concept of the word, thus we adopted the term as our seal.

From the beginning we were anxious to develop new styles and work in our own way. However, sometimes when working for a third party, we are more or less bound by many things. Now, we try to balance between the two and always try to go ahead with our own ideas whenever the situation allows.

– How would you describe your design process?

We usually work in a very flowing way, as we make some rough sketches and take in a lot of references before working on something new — color palettes, styles, finishing, etc. We are so simple at this point that we use mostly a pencil and some markers. We love to simplify the process, thus we draw it manually and finish it on the computer. However, sometimes we also work directly on the computer with Illustrator or Photoshop, depending on the specifications of the project, like textile, motion or editorial. All in all, we adapt every project to the desired workflow.

– What would you say about your design style?

For us, we are not looking for a "design style," as we think it boring to do the same thing all the time. We struggle to achieve different results based on the actual project needs, so we try to explore different techniques and new styles as much as possible. By this we mean that next time when you see other works, you will try to analyze and identify in your mind how that graphic could be done and what you would do in that situation.

– The character designs of your project YUDANSHA Monsters & Masters are very intriguing. Where do you get your inspiration?

Thank you so much. We are happy that you like it. Since this collection was developed for a JiuJitsu brand, in

the beginning we decided to center on old Japanese Samurai wood block engravings, which are amazing for their style, lines, movement, and colors. We took this inspiration to form images of the demons, skulls, fire, swords, etc. And then we broadened our vision by adding some new elements and details like UFOs. Overall, we tried to achieve that unique feeling of wood block engravings.

– How do you usually choose the color scheme for a specific project? Let's take your project NEFF Headwear for example.

This project was a kids collection for a streetwear brand, so we realized that bright colors would fit perfectly. The palette applied to that type of graphics should make them bolder and create a high visual impact. Thus, we decided to take reference from the fantastic works of Jack Kirby and Will Sweeney, and came up with these types of color combos.

– Do you have any advice for designers and illustrators who aspire to enter the world of streetwear?

We think that a designer's vision could take a brand to the next level or take it to hell. We need to try to be more daring and honest, and never be afraid of taking the risk of trying something new. We always say that we are not one to give advice. Everyone has his/her own situation and way of thinking, but overall we have to be honest with ourselves.

You should try to do whatever you are good at and fight for what you want to be. This is a long-distance race. The least you should do is put all of you heart into it so that you do not regret anything or feel tired.

We love a quote from the movie *Cloud Atlas*: "You have to do whatever you can't not do."

– What else are you keen on besides design?

We love family, friends, films, TV series, eating, drinking, and enjoying life.

– What is your motto?

We do not struggle to be different, we strive to be ourselves. Spread love.

YUDANSHA FIGHTWEAR —
Monsters & Masters

- **DESIGN AGENCY**
  Valístika Studio
- **CLIENT**
  YUDANSHA

Valístika Studio was commissioned by YUDANSHA, a combat sportswear company based in Florida, US, to develop a special collection inspired by martial arts spirituality. Valístika decided to go one step further and try to create a collection inspired by Japanese culture with some actual details.

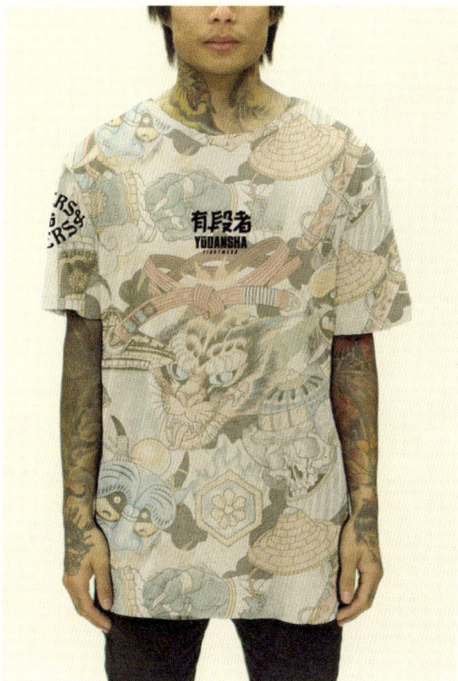 

FRONT

BACK

FRONT

BACK

LIKE CHEESE
ON MACARONI

•DESIGN AGENCY
Valístika Studio
•ART DIRECTION
Michele Salati

Valístika was asked to take part in the project "LIKE CHEESE ON MACARONI," which means a perfect fit. To refine the image of a typical Italian product — SANGUE DI GIUDA, also known as Judas' blood, they decided to represent Judas' image with a rope on his neck and 30 coins in his hand. Inspired by an old legend that Judas became a vampire after his betrayal of Christ, which was regarded as the prototype of vampires, Valístika chose a color palette of red and black to give the graphic a dark and mysterious look.

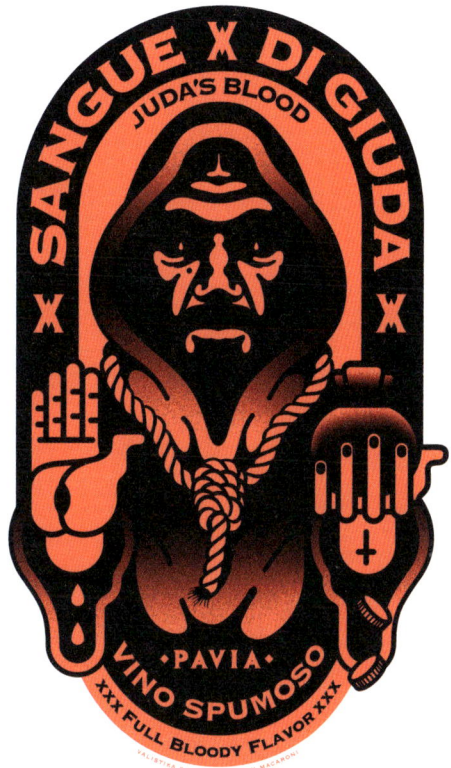

NEFF HEADWEAR

- **DESIGN AGENCY**
  Valístika Studio
- **ART DIRECTION**
  Beau Lawrence, Chelsea Almquist
- **CLIENT**
  NEFF

The NEFF team asked Valístika to create a collection of graphics. They tried hard to achieve several graphic styles in a visual mixture. They came up with two solutions, the Bad Kids Club and Damian Marley collections. The first one applied African iconography to the graphics and used powerful colors to give greater visual impact.

Another solution was to create a collection in collaboration with NEFF and Damian Marley. The idea was to develop a complete collection reflecting Damian's style along with a series of icons inspired by some recurrent concepts: music, respect, peace, death, crowns, lions and marijuana, etc.

▲ Bad Kids Club Collection

NEFF
MISTY
DAMIAN MARLEY

NEFF
MISTY
DAMIAN MARLEY

DAMIAN MARLEY
NEFF

▲ Damian Marley Collection

Sam Dunn

Sam Dunn is a freelance illustrator based in East London. Her work is delicately crafted by hand with pen and ink and colored digitally with many layers of textures, which aims to preserve the warm and tangible appearance of traditional media.

INTERVIEW

– What originally drove you to become an illustrator?

I always loved drawing from a very young age so it was a natural choice for me to pursue this as my career. After high school, I went to Central Saint Martins College of Art and Design to study Graphic Design and Illustration.

– How would you describe your design process? What materials do you enjoy working with the most?

I usually start by making a rough sketch digitally using a Wacom tablet. Once the sketch has been finalized, I print it out in a very light blue color so that I can use ink over it. Then, I remove the original sketch when the line work is complete and scan it back to my computer. After that I clean up the line work and start adding color digitally. For all 3D pieces like my custom shoes, I always use a Sharpie marker; for ink drawings on paper I use a Pentel Pocket Brush pen.

– How would you describe your work style?

Intricate lines, bright colors, lots of details. I like drawing by hand. Even though it is usually faster to draw digitally now, there is something I enjoy about drawing on paper.

– Where do you usually get inspiration?

I get inspired by lots of things, especially nature. I guess most figures in my work are just an extension of my love of nature. There are also many influences coming together, from the wallpaper prints of the Arts and Crafts movement to skateboarding, punk, wood cuts, linocut art, street art, folk art, and folklore, etc. Living in London for the last eight years has also had a huge effect on me as a person and naturally on the things I am producing.

– In your opinion, what role do graphic design and illustration play in streetwear, like apparel, shoes, headwear, and so on?

They play a huge role as they are all intertwined. All brands have their own distinct aesthetic, which would not exist without a strong foundation of graphic design.

– Do you have any advice for illustrators who aspire to enter the world of streetwear?

I do not think I have any direct advice as I do not think I have fully entered the world of streetwear myself. Some of my projects have dipped into this world, like the custom boots, shoes, patches, and snapbacks, but beyond that there are so many more fields to get into which I have never approached. So if I have any advice, I would say that you should try to build good connections, create a product that is on trend, make a plan for longevity, and work hard for sure, which would be the way forward.

– What else are you keen on besides design?

I love playing drums. I have an electronic set at home that I regularly play in between working on my projects. I also love cycling, and I tried racing some track cycling events at my local velodrome. But these days I prefer photographing the event rather than racing in it, which leads me to my other passion — photography.

– Do you have a motto?

I do not think I have a specific motto, other than that in general I try to be kind to people, work hard, and worry less.

ADIDAS SUPERSTAR

A pair of hand-drawn trainers with Sharpie markers.

•**DESIGN & ILLUSTRATION**
 Sam Dunn
•**PHOTOGRAPHY**
 Sam Dunn

Caterpillar
Colorado Boots

- **DESIGN & ILLUSTRATION**
  Sam Dunn
- **ILLUSTRATION AGENCY**
  Blink Art
- **CREATIVE AGENCY**
  Canoe Inc.
- **CLIENT**
  Caterpillar
- **PHOTOGRAPHY**
  Sam Dunn

The Custom Caterpillar boots were designed for the 25th anniversary of the Colorado. Sam Dunn drew directly onto the surface of the boots with Sharpie markers.

SOULSHAKER69 CAP

•DESIGN & ILLUSTRATION
Sam Dunn
•CLIENT
Soulshaker69

Sam Dunn designed the repeated pattern for the snapback caps of the streetwear brand, Soulshaker69. The pattern was hand drawn, then scanned and edited digitally, and finally, printed onto fabric.

Patches & Pins

•**DESIGN & ILLUSTRATION**
Sam Dunn
•**PHOTOGRAPHY**
Sam Dunn

A range of patches and pins designed and produced
for various brands and promotional giveaways.

BANDIT-1$M Collection

•DESIGN & ILLUSTRATION
123KLAN

BANDIT-1$M is a clothing brand established by 123KLAN. They design their own streetwear under the influence and inspiration of 90's graffiti art in Europe and New York. Their works are enriched by huge, sharp-angled letters in acid colors and characters with futuristic manga features alongside experimental type.

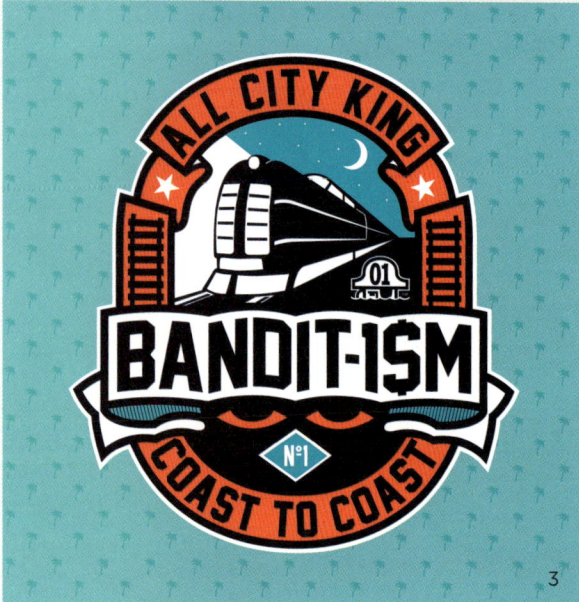

1-4 BANDIT-1$M Spring / Summer

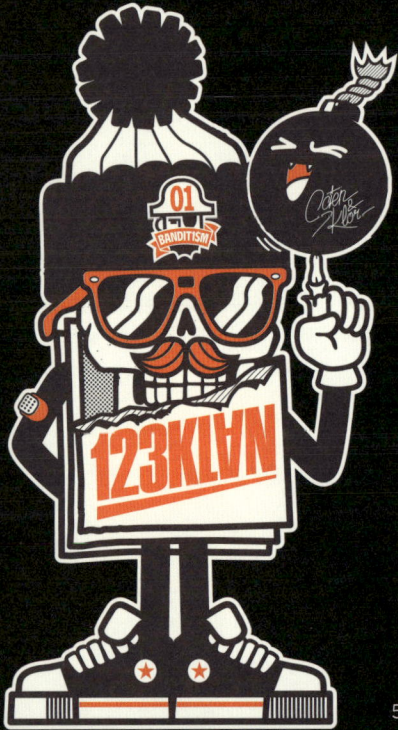

5

MY LIFE MY RULES

6

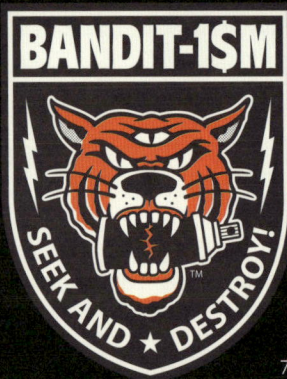

BANDIT-1$M

SEEK AND ★ DESTROY!

7

BANDIT1$M
MY LIFE MY RULES
01
MTL

8

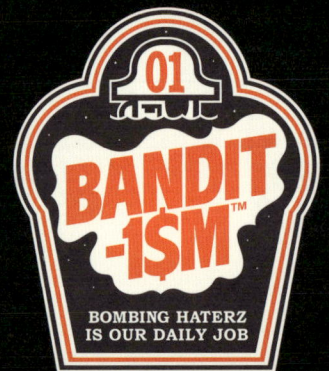

01

BANDIT
-1$M™

BOMBING HATERZ
IS OUR DAILY JOB

9

5-9   BANDIT-1$M Winter

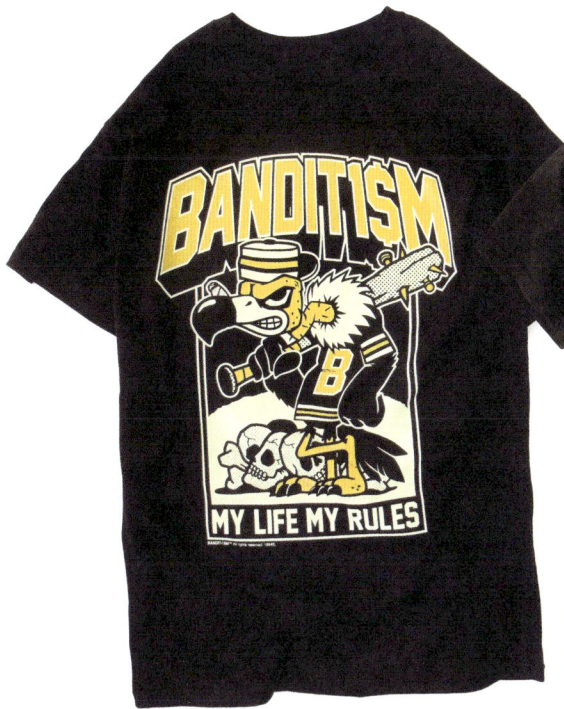

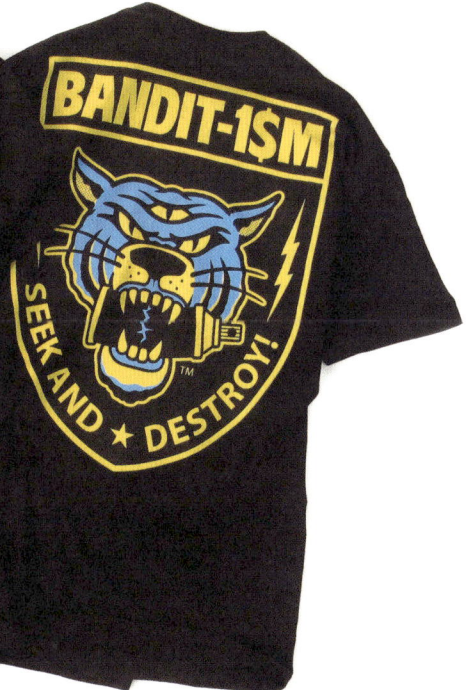

Die Like a Crude

•**DESIGN & ILLUSTRATION**
  Bnomio
•**ART DIRECTION**
  Bnomio
•**Client**
  Crude
•**PHOTOGRAPHY**
  Juanma Jmse

Die Like a Crude is a capsule collection in collaboration with Crude Clothing Brand and Bnomio. It is inspired by old school skate culture. Aside from T-shirts, the collection also includes key chains and coffee mugs.

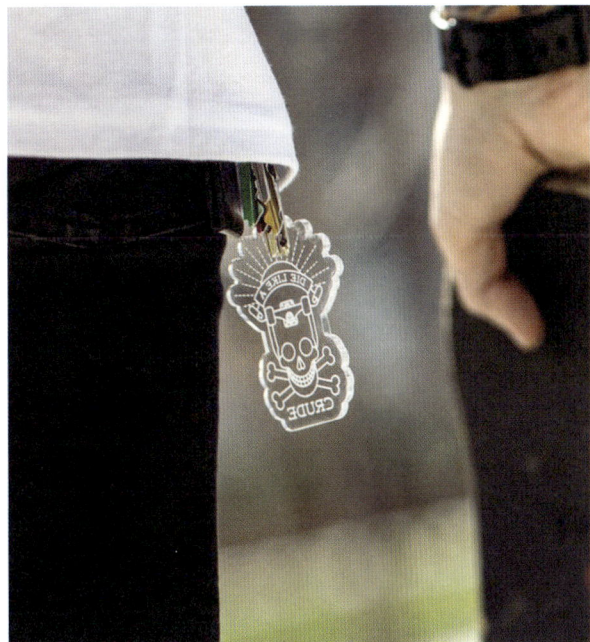

Drawing in L.A. Collection

•**DESIGN & ILLUSTRATION**
 Gabriel Holzner (Gabe)
•**PHOTOGRAPHY**
 Kerstin Rothkopf

Drawing in L.A. is a personal series of graphic artworks, which are influenced by the city of Los Angeles. Gabriel Holzner also used the graphics for his first GABE apparel collection.

Bring The Noise

•**DESIGN & ILLUSTRATION**
Simón Londoño Sierra (Le Monsta)

This is a series of patterns and illustration for textile applications inspired by zombies, 90's hip hop culture, and urban sports.

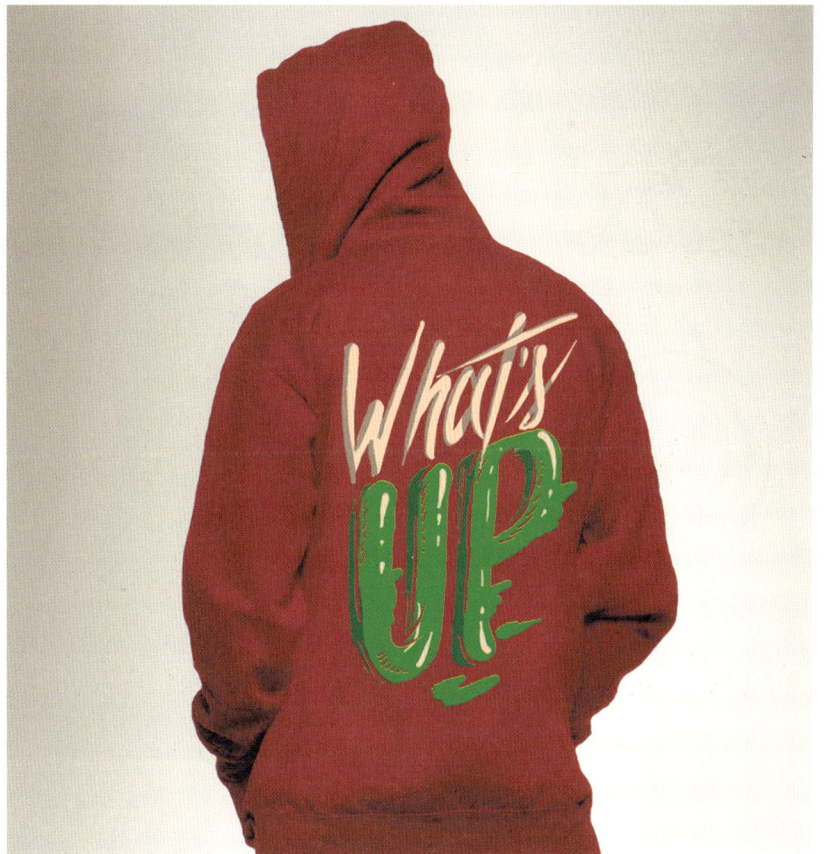

SEEN X Amount of Niceness Project

•**DESIGN & ILLUSTRATION**
  Gabriel Holzner (Gabe)
•**CREATIVE DIRECTION**
  Tobias Huber, Gabriel Holzner

SEEN is a streetwear brand that offers all kinds of apparel under the theme of Jamaican popular culture. For the label's tenth anniversary, the brand released one new SEEN product each month. People would have a ten day period to pre-order the product. Gabriel Holzner was responsible for the design of each item to be released.

Velmost West Coast

•**DESIGN & ILLUSTRATION**
Alejandro Giraldo
•**PHOTOGRAPHY**
Juan Silva

This is a Spring/Summer collection for Velmost. It is inspired by three rival gangs: the San Francisco Mad Seagulls, the Ocean Beach Pirate Whales, and the Surfer Bones from Los Angeles.

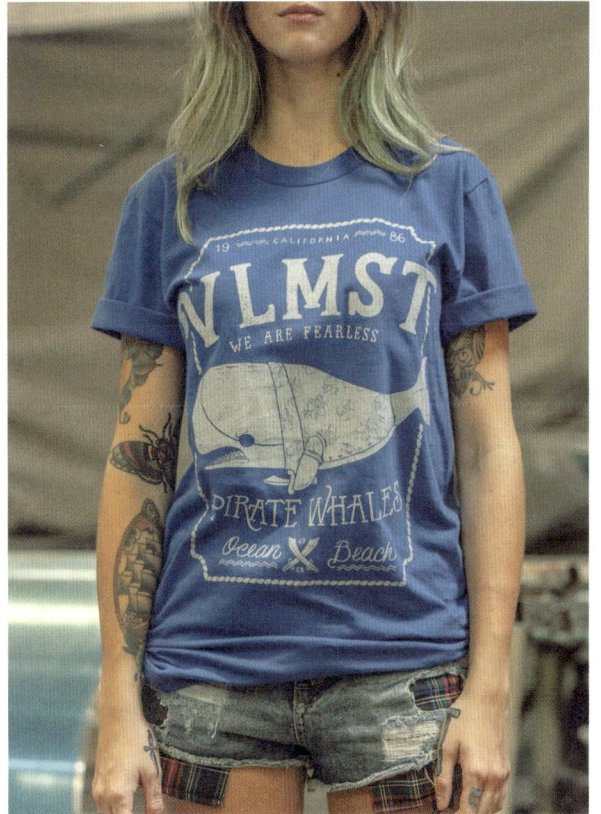

Beleberda X Magicdust
Dresses & Unisex T-shirts

- **DESIGN & ILLUSTRATION**
  Akvilė Magicdust
- **CLIENT**
  Beleberda
- **PHOTOGRAPHY**
  Vaida Tamošauskaitė

- **MODELS**
  Agnė, Greta, Jonas,
  Matas, Zbigniev
- **MAKE UP ARTIST**
  Kristina Raulinaitytė

The patterns show evil cats, gray block houses, teepees, tigers, burning cars, a girl with bleeding knees, haters, love, and bags of money — a balance of positive and negative memes from daily life. Like most of the younger generation, local people grew up in one of the gray block districts in Vilnius, Lithuania. The surroundings may be dull, but the illustrator thinks that the grayness of the outside triggered her imagination to create a positive interior world.

LINDA

•DESIGN & ILLUSTRATION
Andrés Yeah
•CLIENT
Guillermina Nü
•PHOTOGRAPHY
Kimi Neptune

An array of illustrations for Guillermina Nü's Spring/Summer 2016 Campaign.

Boombox Illustrations

•**DESIGN & ILLUSTRATION**
Oscar Fernández

Boombox is a project inspired by the 80's and the designer's regard for pop culture which he employs through the use of limited 8-bit arcade colors, synthetic fabrics, and icons such as pop music, and the *Gremlins*. At first, Oscar conceived this project for T-shirt stamps, but then the project expanded to general clothing, like hoodies, tanks, accessories, hats, socks, etc. His aim is to reinterpret 80's pop culture with a modern twist.

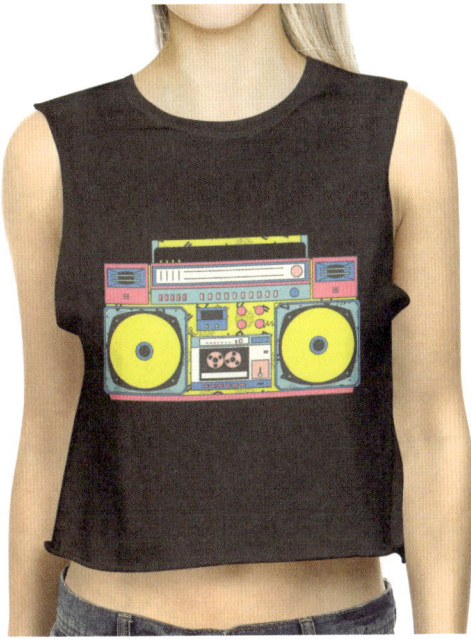

Up the City

- **DESIGN & ILLUSTRATION**
  Cristobal Ojeda (Newfren)
- **CLIENT**
  Up the City

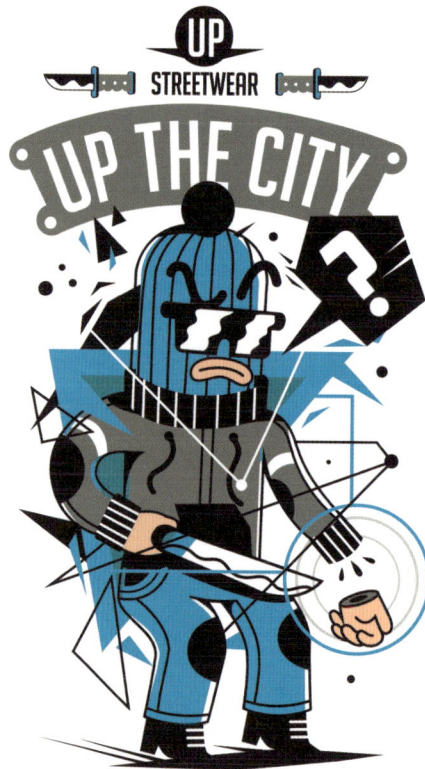

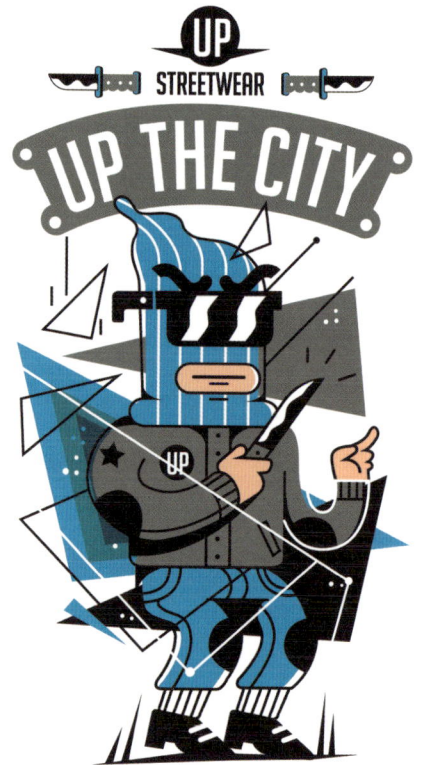

Capsules & Collections

A set of four character designs for a
streetwear brand from Chile called Up
the City. The collection includes T-shirts,
caps, and skateboards in funky styles.

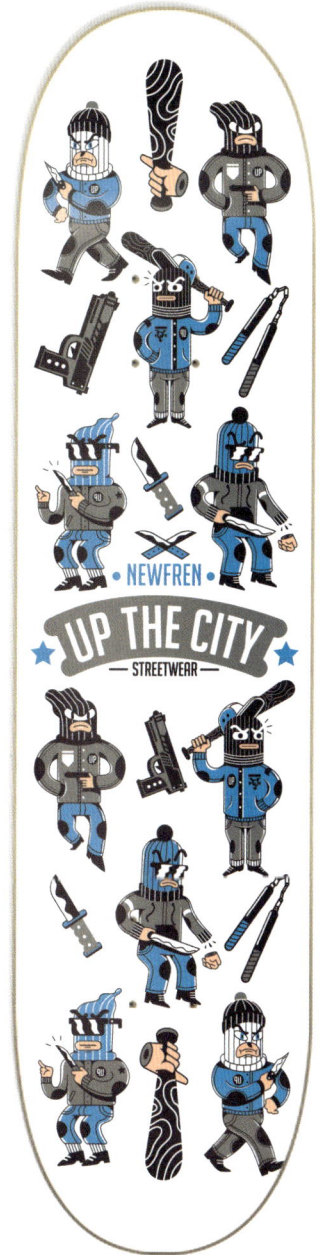

Il Mazzo di Carte

•**DESIGN AGENCY**
 Isoì
•**DESIGN & ART DIRECTION**
 Daniele Desperati
•**ILLUSTRATION**
 Gaia Bernasconi

Il Mazzo di Carte is a
capsule collection. The
whole collection is inspired
by tarot cards.

The Characters

•DESIGN & ILLUSTRATION
Elena Gorbunova
•CLIENT
Lena Vral` Store
•PHOTOGRAPHY
Katerina Guslenko

The Characters is a collection of linocut hand printed T-shirts and canvas tote bags with original designs for the Lena Vral` Store. This limited collection is for those who appreciate unique individual styles.

Seamless Pattern: Minsk

•**DESIGN & ILLUSTRATION**
  Volga Ilyina
•**PHOTOGRAPHY**
  Volga Ilyina

This pattern was inspired by the city that Volga Ilyina loves most — Minsk, where she studied and lived. This city gave her new friends, a sense of freedom, creativity, and priceless experiences. Such passion drove her to make a little present for the city, that is, a seamless pattern. Viewers can see many interesting details of Minsk, such as the metro token, the famous confectionary brand Slodych, the Red Church, and so on.

Eukaryon

•DESIGN & ILLUSTRATION
Simón Londoño Sierra (Le Monsta)

Made for textile applications, this pattern and illustration is composed of dinosaur skulls and tropical forest flora, forming a harmonic composition. All the drawings were inked delicately by hand with Photoshop for the final touches.

Freitag — Design A Truck Competition

•DESIGN & ILLUSTRATION
Isabella Ahmadzadeh

Freitag bags are made from recycled materials, of which the main component is truck tarps. For the Freitag — Design A Truck Competition, Isabella Ahmadzadeh created two illustrations for the side tarps. Being a fan of Freitag since her adolescence, Isabella put all her imagination into this project, which turned out to be the idea of a colorful and crazy Freitag Factory. These illustrations have been featured by Freitag in the shortlist of the 40 best proposals for the Freitag — Design A Truck Competition.

Emil Boards:
Artist Series

- **DESIGN & ILLUSTRATION**
  Gabriel Holzner (Gabe)
- **ART DIRECTION**
  Niklas Groschup
- **PHOTOGRAPHY**
  Niklas Groschup

This is a special artist edition for Munich-based skateboard brand, Emil Boards. Gabriel Holzner created some handmade illustrations for this brand's T-shirts, skateboards, and art prints.

Clothing & Shoes for MaïProject

•**DESIGN & ILLUSTRATION**
 Natalia Zerko
•**CLIENT**
 MaïProject

MaïProject is a French brand of shoes with a unique social engagement. Wearing MaïProject means being part of a story — for each pair of MaïProject shoes purchased, 2 euros are given to a specific cause within a humanitarian project.

For this project, the participating designers were allowed to choose the theme of drawing. The textile shoes were hand-drawn with acrylic paint and Uni Posca pens. The main idea behind Natalia Zerko's drawing was the fetters of adulthood.

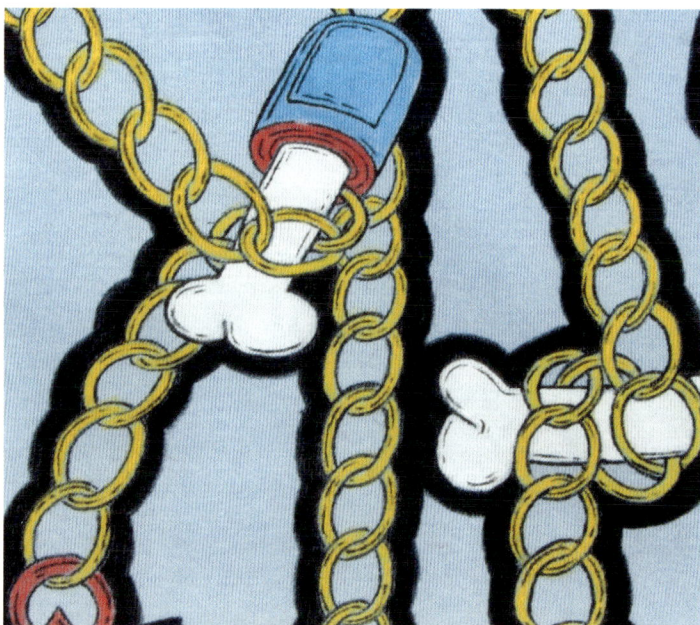

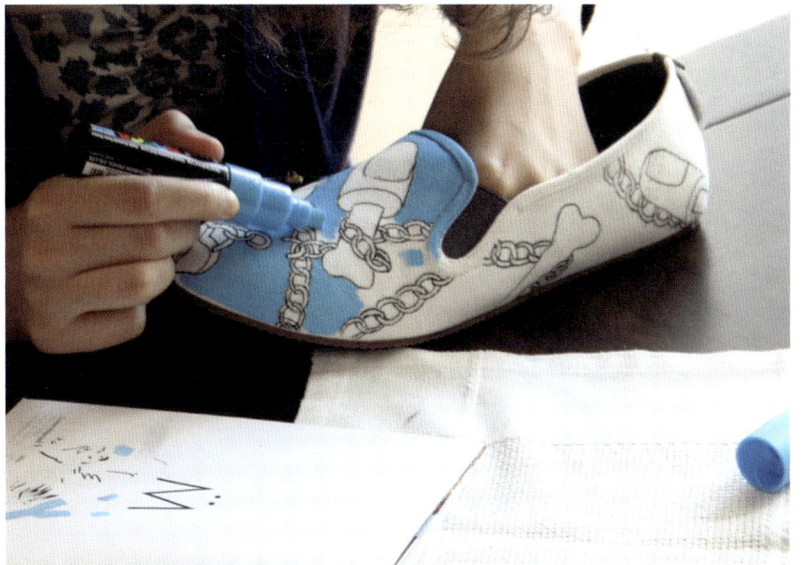

GARAND BRAND
MERCH

•**DESIGN & ILLUSTRATION**
 Jakub Rafael
•**CLIENT**
 Garand Brand

Various clothing collections for the fashion label GARAND BRAND.

Logos & Badges

•DESIGN & ILLUSTRATION
  Alexander Shimanov

A collection of logos, badges, and apparel prints for various Russian streetwear brands in a retro, Soviet style.

МАНЬПУПУНЁР
РЕСПУБЛИКА КОМИ

1

RESISTANCE IS FUTILE
EVIL MARTIANS
EVL MS
2006

2

Автолюбитель

3

СЫКТЫВКАР · УСИНСК · ВОРКУТА · УХТА · ПЕЧОРА · ИНТА
РЕСПУБЛИКА
КОМИ
KOMI REPUBLIC
ESTD 1921

4

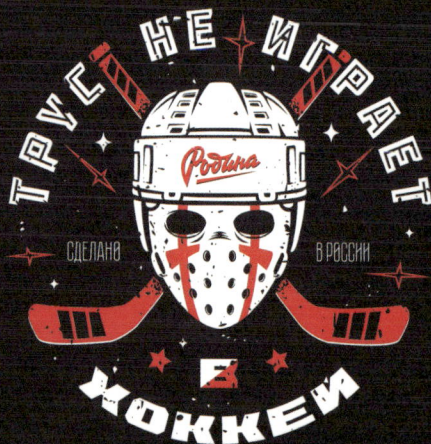

ТРУС НЕ ИГРАЕТ
Родина
СДЕЛАНО   В РОССИИ
В
ХОККЕЙ

5

6

7

8

9

10

Freesundays for BlackMouth Co.

•**DESIGN & ILLUSTRATION**
Luiso Mostacho
•**CLIENT**
BlackMouth Co.
•**PHOTOGRAPHY**
Yaneva Santana, Solecker

Freesundays is part of the Dreamer Club Collection for BlackMouth Co., one of the very first collections of this brand. Freesundays includes screen-printed tote bags and T-shirts. It is the purest representation of the style of Luiso Mostacho.

HELL'S SOUNDTRACK

BLACKMOUTH
—— EST. 2014 ——
CLOTHING CO.

MKNK Hoodies & Snapbacks

•DESIGN & ILLUSTRATION
Derin Ciler

Hoodies, snapbacks, and sticker pack designs for MKNK Clothing, a streetwear brand founded by Derin Ciler.

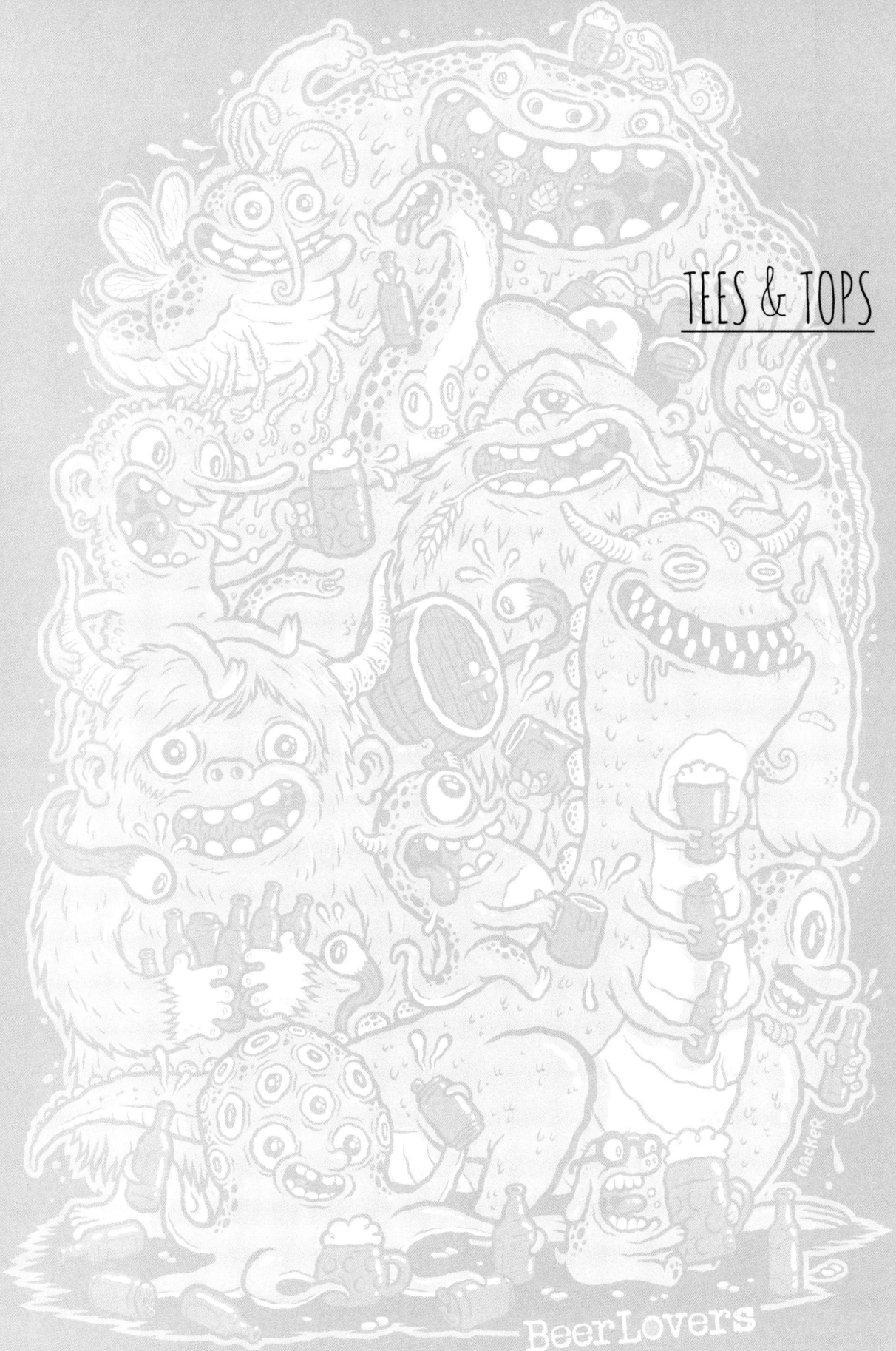

TEES & TOPS

BeerLovers

COLOGNE & HANNOVER

PRESSURE & INK

SCREENPRINTING

Sebastian Mueller

Born in the 1980's, Sebastian Mueller is a graphic designer and illustrator from Cologne, Germany. His work is focused on art direction, brand identity, graphic design, and illustration. In 2015, he teamed up with Chris Weiss and founded the Darker Half Cult, their own apparel brand, to express their love for underground music and urban culture.

INTERVIEW

– What originally drove you to become a graphic designer and illustrator?

I would not say there was a point in my life where I thought: "I want to become an illustrator." It was more like a process that resulted from the urge to make a living from what I love. I was always into art and graphic design, especially the 80's skateboard, metal, and punk graphics, and I started drawing at a very young age. After school I did not know what to do and when the local art school turned down my application, I learned the job the hard way by taking an apprenticeship in a design & PR agency. After working different jobs in different bureaus and companies for a couple of years, I decided to go fully freelance in 2012. This was one of the best decisions in my life to this day and hopefully not the end of the story.

– How would you describe your design process? What materials do you enjoy working with the most?

I keep a folder where I collect all the inspiration I get whether it is screenshots, quotes, typefaces or scribbles. When an idea forms in my head I scan through that folder and check if there is anything that would help to make this idea come to life. I normally do not sketch that much and would rather start with a white canvas. Therefore I end up with loads of different approaches and then pick one to finish up. Recently, I have been trying to go back to a more analog way of working, but most of the time I use a Mac in combination with a Wacom tablet.

– In your opinion, what role does graphic design and illustration play in streetwear, like apparel, shoes, socks, headwear, and so on?

In my view, detailed and complex illustrations are not playing a major role in streetwear any more like they used to do in the 80's or 90's. You will still find the odd skull and bones tee, but I think most brands prefer a more subtle and sophisticated approach when it comes to graphic design these days. Clean and small logos, reduced typography, and less printing colors are the way to go; Polar, Palace, and HUF are the living proof of that. When it comes to band merchandise, it is a different story and I think you can do whatever fits the bands' image and taste.

– How would you define the style of your works for Darker Half Cult?

I think the style of my designs for Darker Half changed a bit over the last year. When my partner Chris Weiss and I started Darker Half in early 2015, it was a way to release all the unused and unwanted graphics that we had in our drawers. Back then, my style was heavily inspired by 80's and 90's skate art. Over the time my designs got a bit cleaner and less complex. They are still very dark and I still love occult imagery, but they are more under the influence of traditional tattoo art than of skateboarding and pop art.

– Images of dark themes are often seen in your works, where do you usually get inspiration?

Mostly from other illustrators and traditional tattooers, but it could be anything from music and magazines to photographs, books, and Instagram.

– What would you consider to be your proudest achievement so far in your design career? What are your goals for the future?

It is still one of the best things to create artworks for bands and brands you admire. Designing tour merchandise for Bad Religion was a huge thing for me. Seeing people wearing my designs, whether it is merchandise for bands or something from the Darker Half range, makes me smile and pushes me to keep creating, reminding me of why I love my job so much.

Personally, my goals for the future are to get better at screen printing and creating websites and to get back to drawing a bit more. Businesswise, I am looking forward to get some new jobs and clients to keep the freelance going and work on some fun projects.

Right now we are planning a couple of new tees and screen prints for Darker Half, which should be out soon. And it would be cool to host our own art show in the next couple of months.

– Do you have any advice for illustrators who aspire to enter the world of streetwear?

Work hard, stay original, and do not sell yourself cheap. It is okay to copy one's art while you are still learning but over the years you should develop your own style and try to improve it. Also, it is great when you are still in school and your favorite band or brand pays you 50 bucks to print your design on a tee (I probably would have done it for free though), but you should remember that good work should have its price and one day you might want to make a living from your art. So selling yourself cheap will come back to haunt you in the long run.

– What else are you keen on besides design and your work?

My wife, skateboarding, surfing, and good food, in that order.

Tee Designs for Darker Half Cult

- **DESIGN & ILLUSTRATION**
  Sebastian Mueller, Chris Weiss
- **CLIENT**
  Darker Half Cult
- **PHOTOGRAPHY**
  Niren Mahajan
- **MODEL**
  Philipp Baum

A collection of T-shirt designs for Darker Half Cult, a brand established by Sebastian Mueller and Chris Weiss.

1 Dark Tower by Sebastian Mueller
2 Ritual by Sebastian Mueller
3 Road Crew by Sebastian Mueller
4 Almanach by Sebastian Mueller
5 Devil by Sebastian Mueller

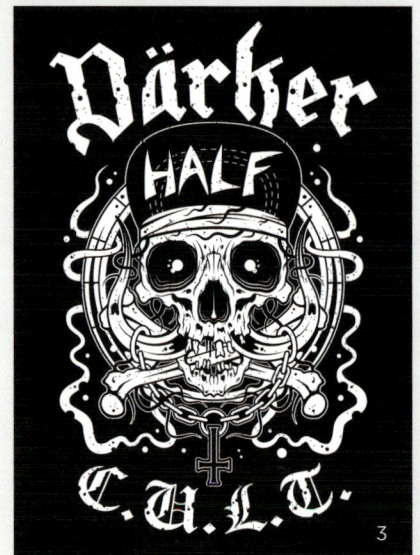

4

5

▲ Death Curse by Chris Weiss

◄ Mind Eraser by Chris Weiss
▼ Lady of Misery by Chris Weiss

Tee Designs for Various Bands

•DESIGN & ILLUSTRATION
Sebastian Mueller

A collection of T-shirt designs for some European and American punk, metal bands.

1 Hysterese
2 Volbeat
3 Die Toten Hosen
4 Bad Religion

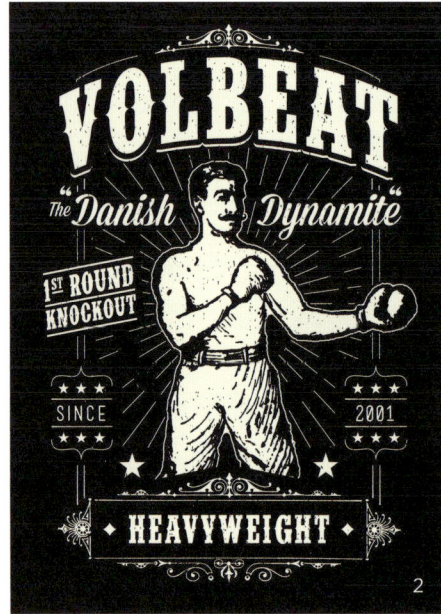

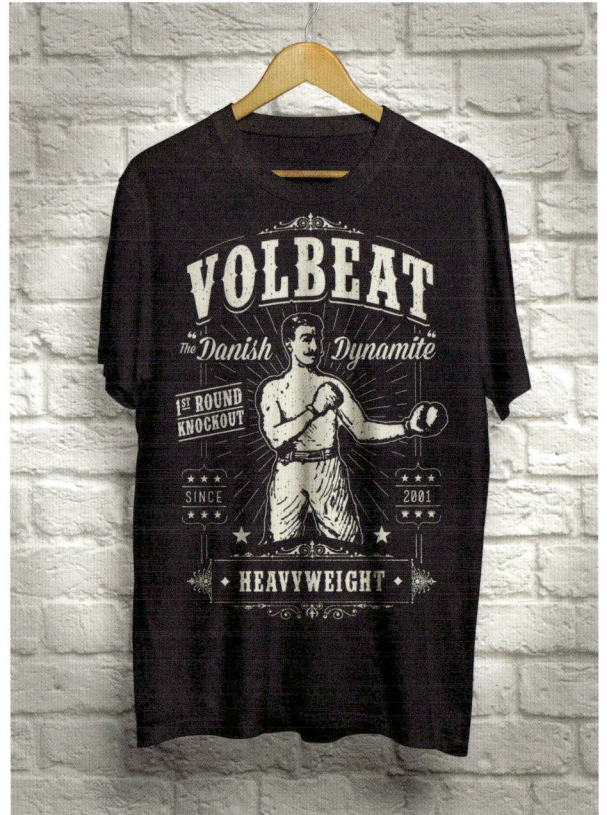

3

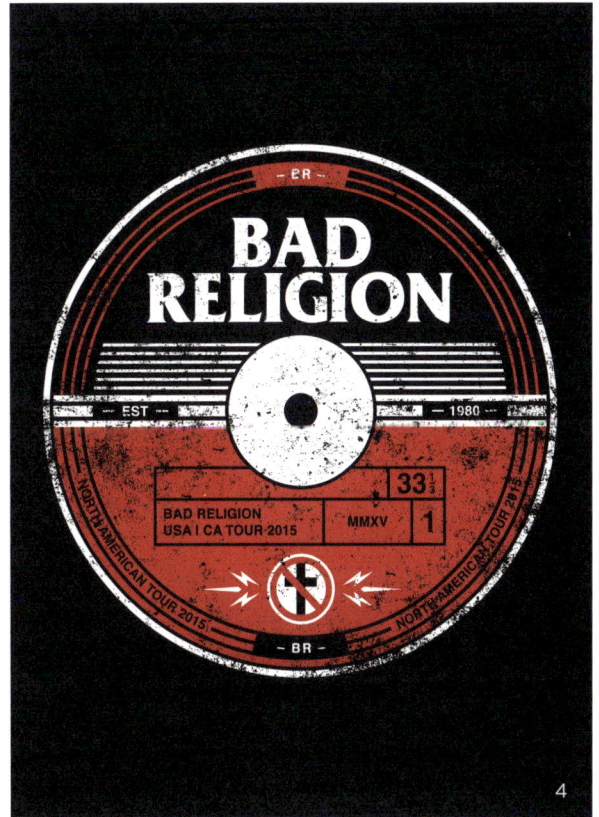

4

Not Anderson

•**DESIGN & ILLUSTRATION**
Pamela Potgieter
•**PHOTOGRAPHY**
Jessie Enslin, Toni-Jayde Louw

Pamela Potgieter has always been interested in fashion, particularly street style, so she created a lifestyle clothing label that reflected her sense of humor and style of illustration. Over the years, Pamela has become increasingly bored of the "Pamela Anderson" jokes that happened when she introduced herself, so she decided to name the brand "Not Anderson," and use the slogan "Less Boob, More Brain." The designs were all illustrated by hand, using pen, ink, gouache paint, and collage, and then digitally printed onto 100% cotton garments.

THE
EVILS OF
ART

A RECIPE

FOR MADNESS

GAME OVER

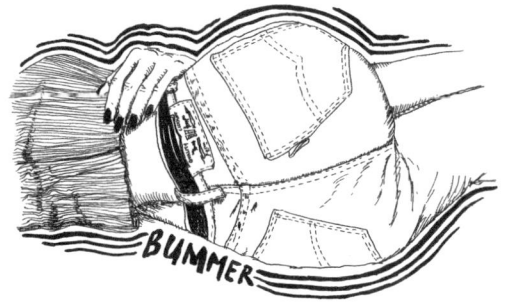

BUMMER

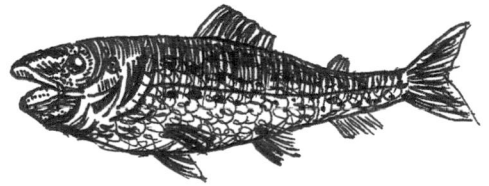

NOT ANDERSON

THE EVILS OF ART

A RECIPE

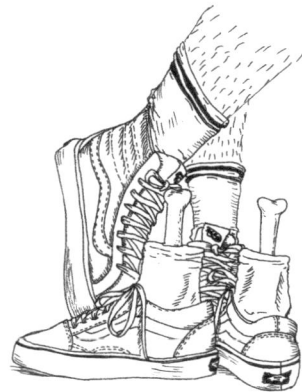

FOR MADNESS

NOT ANDERSON

N/A

Various Illustrations Collection

- **DESIGN AGENCY**
  Mighty Harbour Studio
- **ILLUSTRATION**
  Iqbal Hakim Boo
- **PHOTOGRAPHY**
  Mighty Harbour Studio

A collection of illustrations for some local clothing brands based in Malaysia.

1   Rise of Falco for Thasmoosh
2   Kulcats
3   The Occult for Junkcult
4   Terbang My for Construct Project
5–6   Death Ripper for Thasmoosh
7   Dirty by Nature for Reverse

1

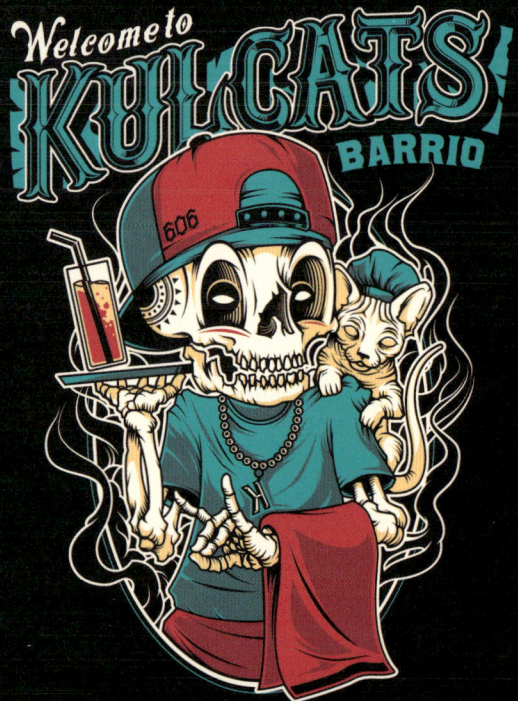

2

3

4

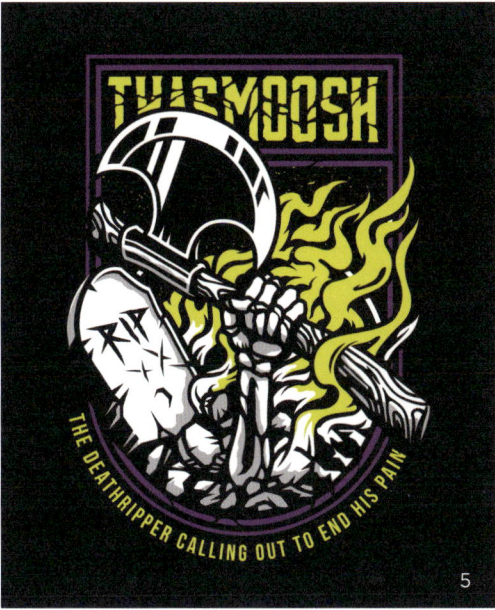

5

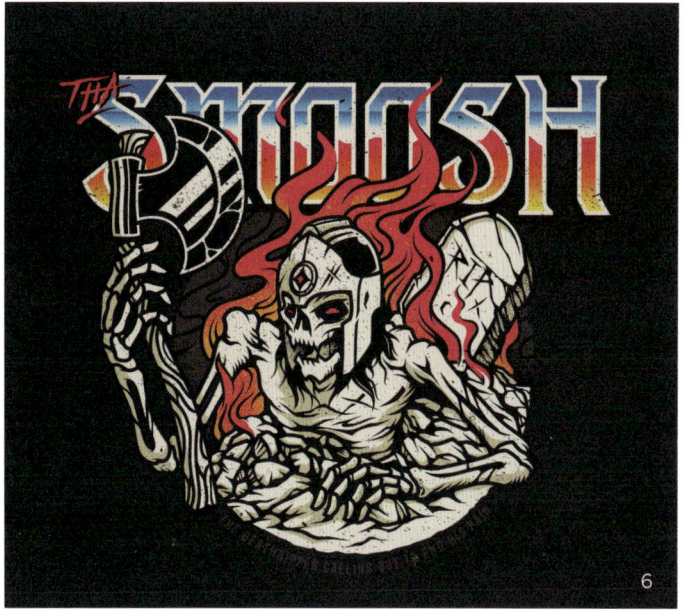

6

7

Kushi Clothing

•DESIGN & ILLUSTRATION
Riccardo Sabatini, Alessandro Landucci

This is a personal clothing project that the designers started a few years ago. Riccardo Sabatini was first commissioned by his partner to do the logo, then they joined forces and followed up by building the brand identity and the T-shirt collection.

KUSHI 鮨 ITALIANSUSHI

SPECIALTY
ITALIAN/MAKIZUSHI
ONLY!!! 480円
GETSUYOUBI 月曜日
GENUINE FOOD CULTURE

KUSHI CLTHNG
K
G × F
C
EST
2013

KUSHICLTHNG
THIS MEANS A BUSHI (WARRIOR) MUST NOT WITHDRAW WHAT HE HAS SAID ONCE

Bushi Ni 武士
NIGON
NASHI
武士に二言無し

IN JAPAN WITHDRAWING A DECISION OR PROMISE
THAT IS SAID ONCE WAS SHAMEFUL AS A SAMURAI.

GOIN GFUR THER

↘ KUSHI CLOTHING   ↘ TRANSLATED * RUST TO THE BLADE

身から出た金青

* RUST TO THE BLADE / Meaning: What comes around goes around.
The 青 in this proverb refers to this blade of a katana. If you don't keep it in good condition it will rust and lose it's usability.
Thus this proverb refers to some negative thing that is happening to a person because of their own poor judgment or actions.

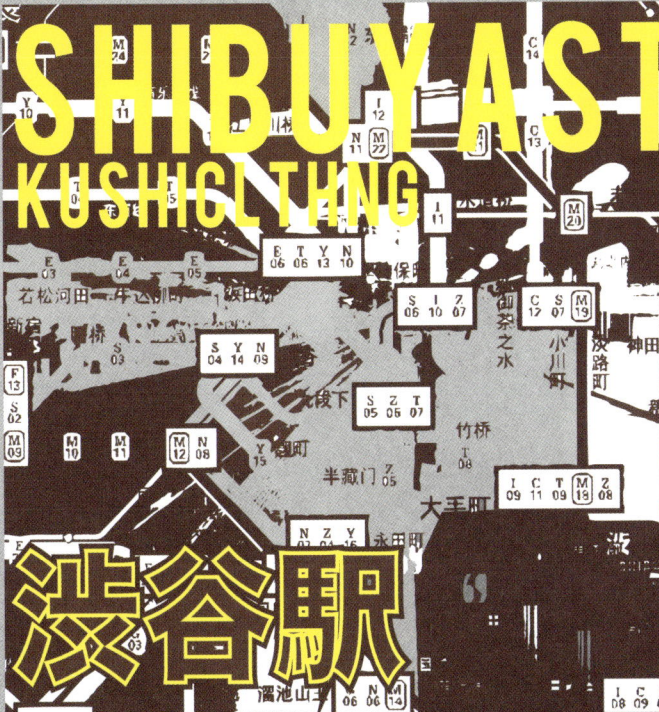

SHIBUYA STATION
KUSHICLTHNG

渋谷駅

SHIBUYA IS SYMBOLIC AS A CENTER OF YOU
THE NORTHWEST SIDE OF SHIBUYA STATION
STRETCHING FROM THE HACHIKO EXIT,
IS THE AREA'S ENTERTAINMENT DISTRICT.
HACHIKO-MAE PLAZA IS PROBABLY THE MOST POPU
MEETING PLACE IN ALL OF JAPAN.

LINE/ 69

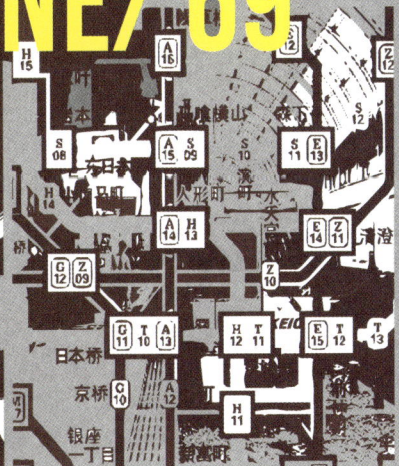

Madlady Clothing

•DESIGN & ILLUSTRATION
Riccardo Sabatini
•CLIENT
Madlady

Riccardo Sabatini designed this capsule collection for a Swedish online fashion store Madlady for their very first apparel collection. The path from the initial development to the final products has been perilous and full of a series of unexpected events like the plot of the movie Zoolander 2. Riccardo spent two months working on this project and kept trying some strange, yet fancy, pop designs to better illustrate the brand.

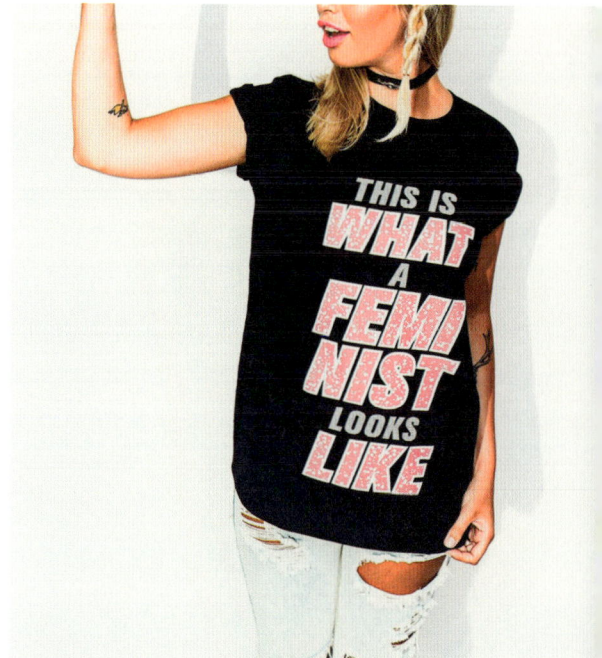

▲ Girl Squad

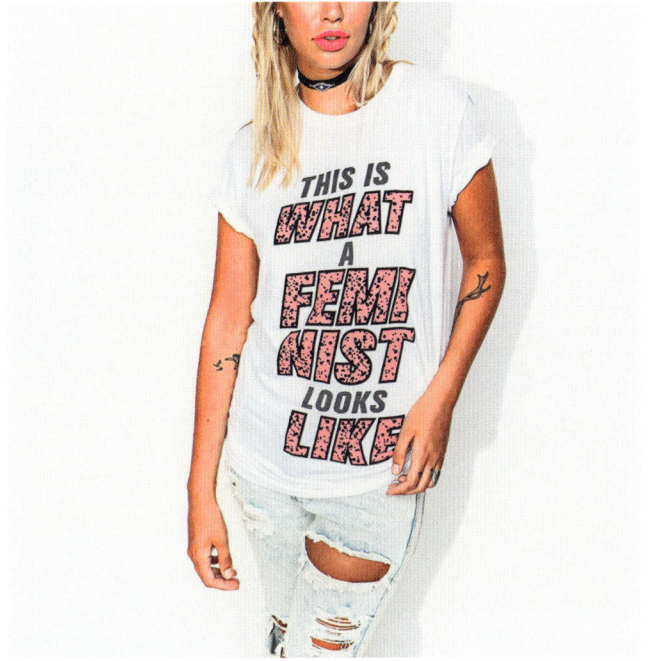

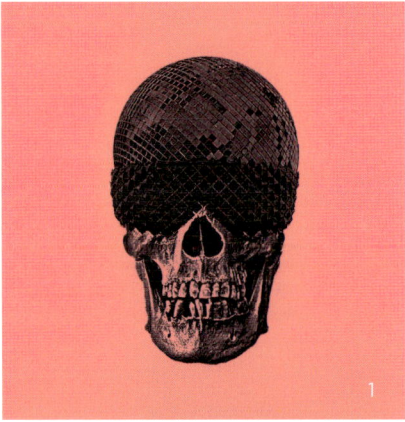

1

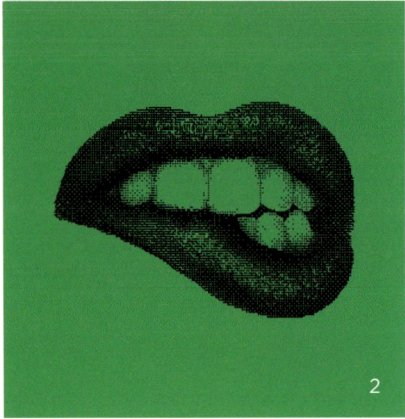

2

3

4

1 Disko Skull
2 Poison Lips
3 Bitch, I'm Fabulous
4 Summer Bomb

Nike Young Athletes X Rusc

•**DESIGN & ILLUSTRATION**
Rubens Scarelli
•**ART DIRECTION**
Christopher DeGaetano
•**CLIENT**
Nike

A set of projects for the Nike
Young Athletes collection (USA).

1 DJ Bad Airs
2 Air Raid
3 Cool Guy Rapper

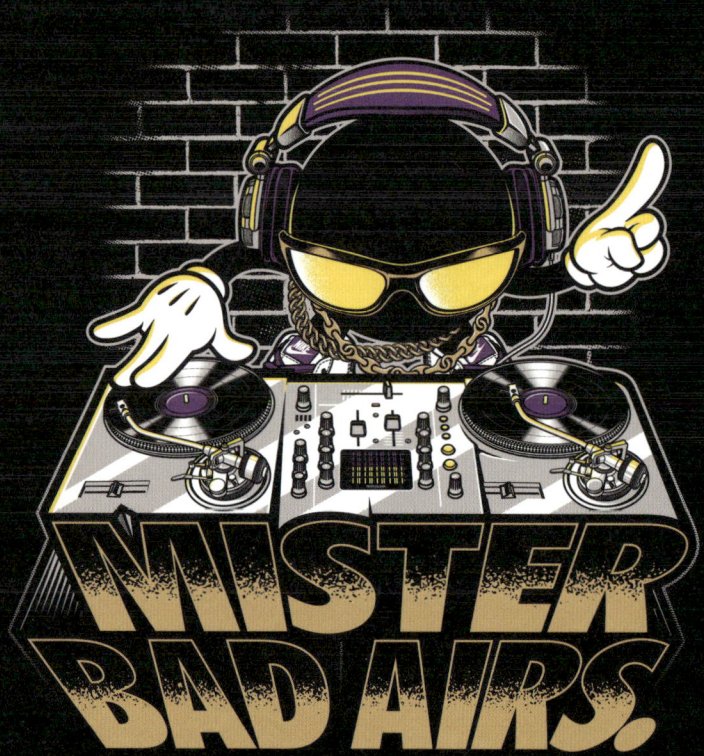

1

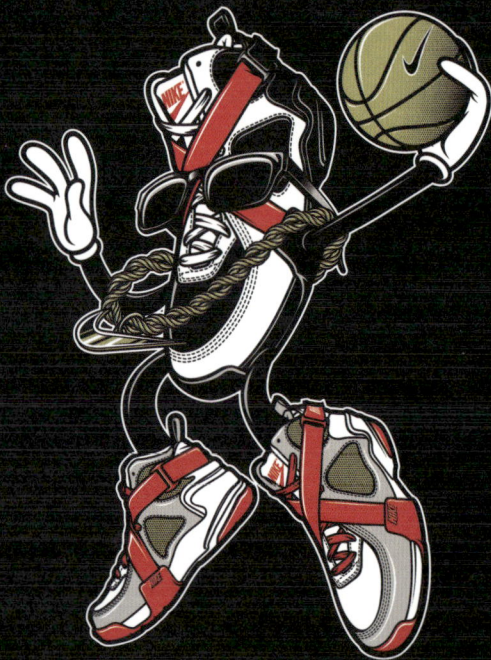

2

3

1

2

1 Forever Fly
2 Octopus Kicks
3 So Fly

IGNAT'EV INK X
Mech Clothing

•**DESIGN & ILLUSTRATION**
 Maxim Ignat'ev (IGNAT'EV INK)
•**PHOTOGRAPHY**
 Mech Clothing

Illustrator Maxim Ignat'ev created some illustrations for the clothing brand Mech Clothing from St. Petersburg. The graphic concept was visualized as abstract mountains in which people stored their thoughts and dreams in bright prints and colors.

Filter017 X
Undergarden 1ST

- **DESIGN AGENCY**
  Filter017
- **DESIGN & ILLUSTRATION**
  Filter017
- **CLIENT**
  Undergarden
- **PHOTOGRAPHY**
  Filter017

Filter017 was invited to collaborate with Undergarden, a famous streetwear shop in Taiwan, for their first anniversary. Filter017 created an amusing and friendly visual image Mr. #1 which is a perfect inspiration for this special occasion and true to the spirit of Undergarden which is grateful for all its supporters. "Pleased to meet you, I am Mr. #1, and happy birthday to Undergarden!" said Mr. #1.

Tees

•DESIGN & ILLUSTRATION
 Mr Woody Woods

A series of illustrations for T-shirts.

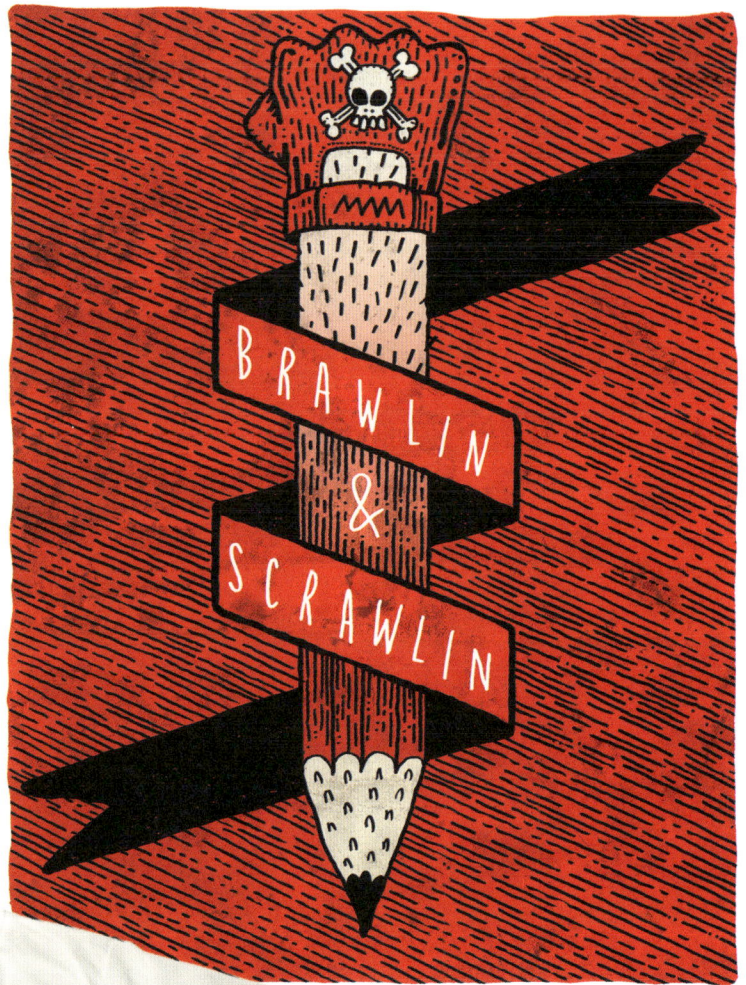

Let's Wrestle

•DESIGN & ILLUSTRATION
Mr Woody Woods

A series of colorful Mexican
wrestler illustrations and
apparel designs.

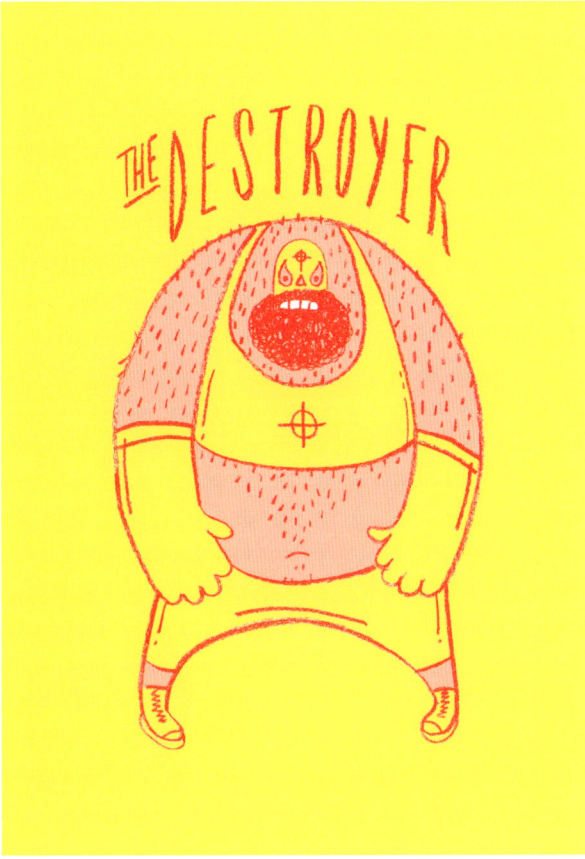

BeerLovers

•**DESIGN & ILLUSTRATION**
Michael Hacker
•**CLIENT**
Beerlovers

T-shirt and beer coaster designed for BeerLovers — Austria's biggest craft beer store located in Vienna. The different creatures in the illustration show the vast diversity of beer styles and beer drinkers.

Adidas Neo
Apparel Design

•**DESIGN & ILLUSTRATION**
Mighty SHORT
•**ART DIRECTION**
Hover Christopher
•**CLIENT**
Adidas Neo

Since 2012, Mighty SHORT
has collaborated with
Adidas Neo on some
t-shirt designs for various
collections.

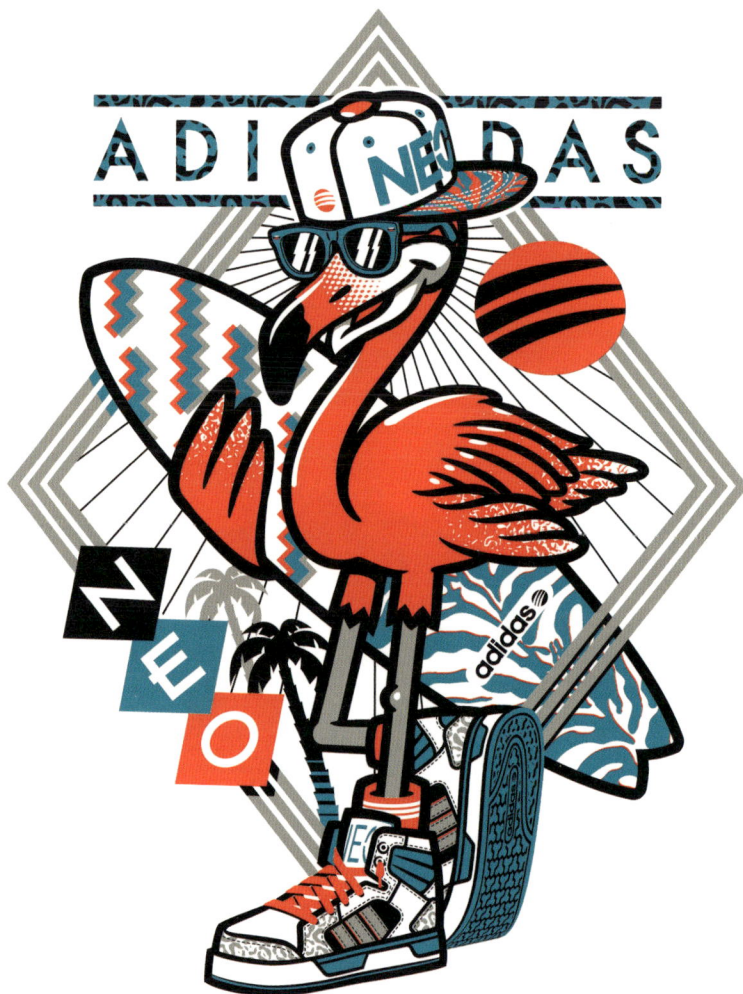

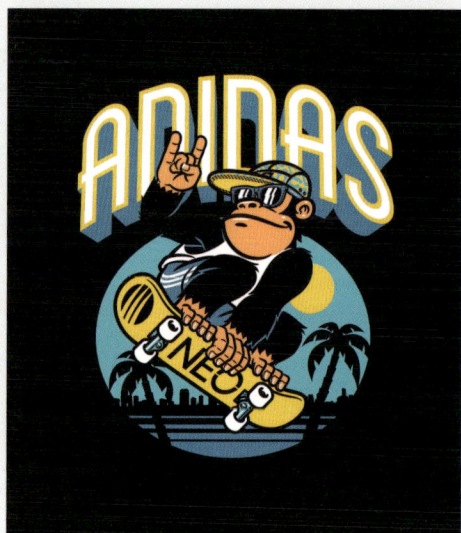

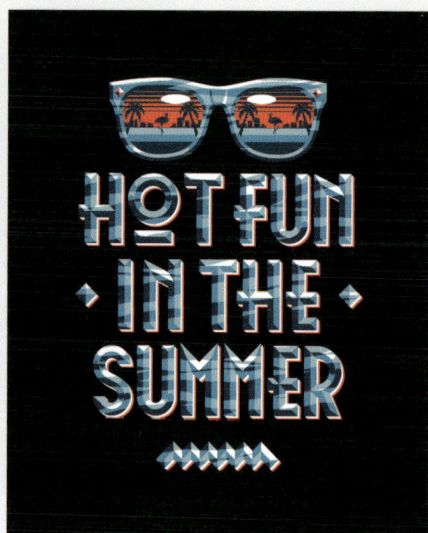

MADBEEF Volume 1 Streetwear

• **DESIGN AGENCY**
Mighty Harbour Studio
• **ART DIRECTION**
Kimy Ordic
• **ILLUSTRATION**
Iqbal Hakim Boo
• **CLIENT**
Mighty Harbour Studio
• **PHOTOGRAPHY**
Mighty Harbour Studio

MADBEEF, a brand owned by Mighty Harbour Studio, is a premium streetwear fashion project for the masses worldwide. Based in Malaysia, Madbeef was initially created to express the local street scenes, sports, and lifestyle trends through a series of illustration artworks. Mainly targeted to fashion-oriented young adults, Mighty Harbour Studio continues to highlight the brand with fresh detailed illustrations. MADBEEF is a green brand campaigning to resolve all the "hating" culture as the designers are mad about all the "beefing" around the community. Their tagline "Beef In Beef Out" means there is no room for beefing here.

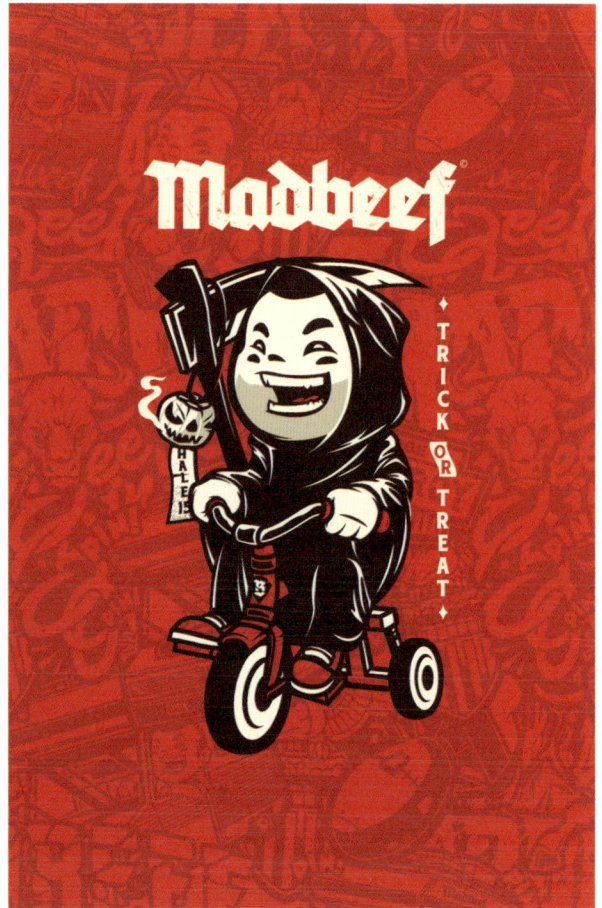

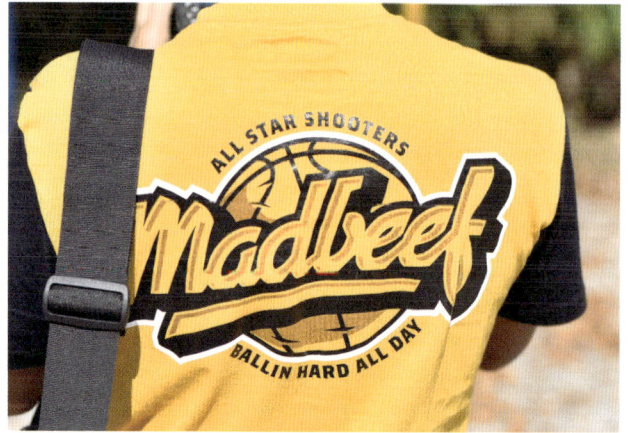

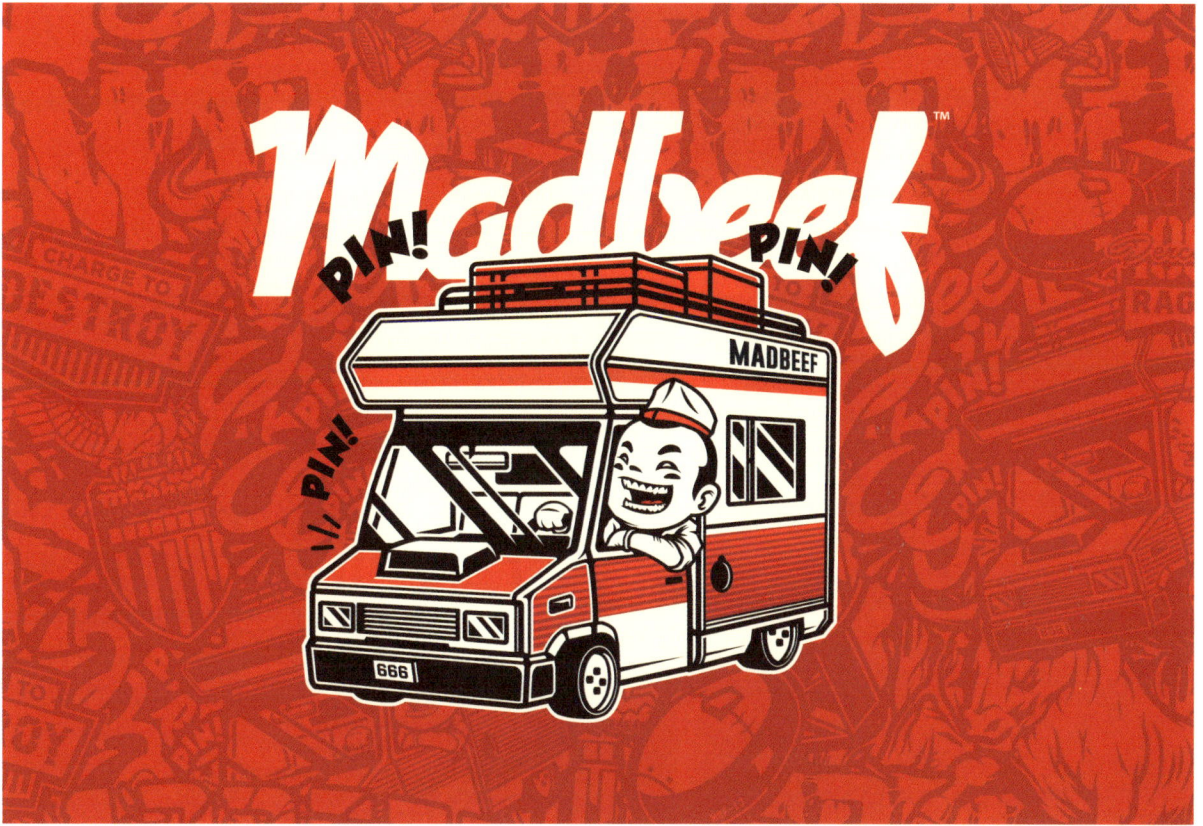

Mighty SHORT X
Reverse Magazine

•ART DIRECTION & ILLUSTRATION
Mighty SHORT
•CLIENT
Reverse Magazine

Reverse, a French bimonthly basketball magazine, asked Mighty SHORT to work on a series of artworks dedicated to the NBA. They chose to work on the "SPLASH BROS," the famous duo from the Warriors composed of the two All-Star players Klay Thompson and Stephen Curry, the comeback of Lebron James to the Cleveland Cavaliers, and on Kobe Bryant, the Black Mamba, from the Los Angeles Lakers. The series includes three designs available on crewneck sweatshirt or T-shirt.

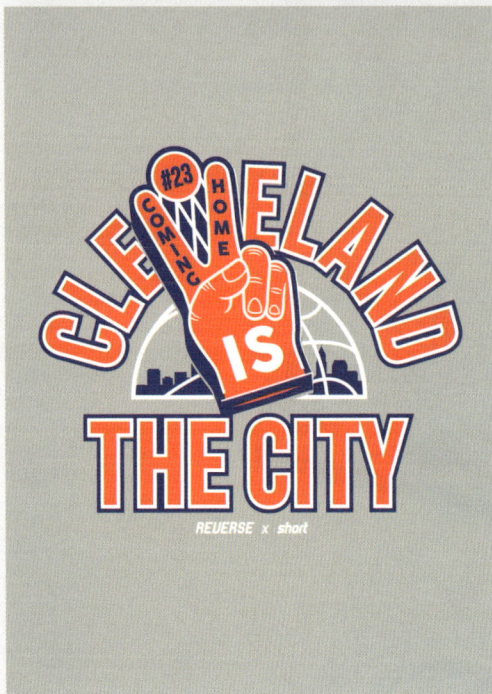

Digital Vandals for Nike

•**DESIGN & ILLUSTRATION**
Why Duck
•**CREATIVE DIRECTION**
Bartłomiej Walczuk (Mr Osom)
•**LETTERING**
Bartłomiej Walczuk (Mr Osom)
•**CLIENT**
Nike
•**PHOTOGRAPHY**
Maksym Rudnik

Why Duck was asked by Nike Poland to deliver a custom Nike's Destroyer Jacket to celebrate their accomplishments as a digital team. The designers created dedicated typography and illustration that reflected the team's field: a shoe lace tied around a tattooed arm, and a disassembled hand holding a smartphone. The desired goal was to make this jacket an instant classic. Why Duck scrolled through many references and found a way to connect Why Duck's cartoon illustrations with Mr Osom's wavy lettering.

VANS T-shirt

•**DESIGN & ILLUSTRATION**
Tianlin Ma
•**CLIENT**
VANS

Abstract lettering design
for VANS T-shirts.

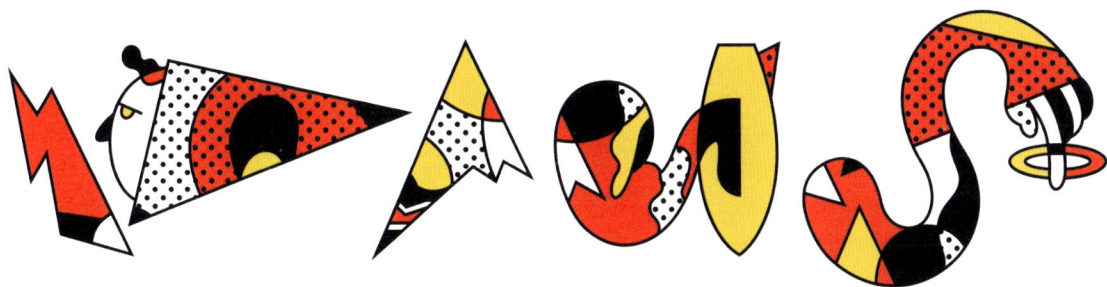

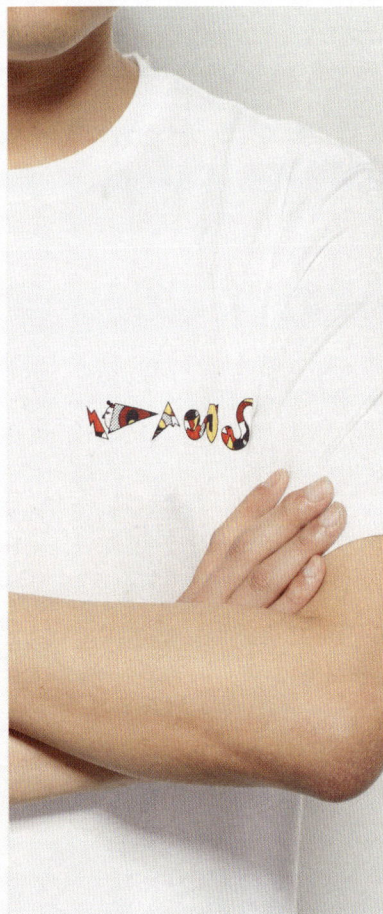

IGNAT'EV INK X
We All Die Young

•**DESIGN & ILLUSTRATION**
Maxim Ignat'ev (IGNAT'EV INK)
•**CLIENT**
We All Die Young
•**PHOTOGRAPHY**
We All Die Young

Illustration of a bat in
Japanese style for the
clothing brand "We All Die
Young" from St. Petersburg.

MKNK X Second Tee

•DESIGN
  Derin Ciler

T-shirt design in collaboration with MKNK Clothing and the punk rock band, Second.

Blackwater
Studios T-shirts

- **DESIGN & ILLUSTRATION**
  Bene Rohlmann
- **CLIENT**
  Blackwater Studios
- **PHOTOGRAPHY**
  Blackwater Studios

T-shirt illustrations
for the British brand
Blackwater Studios.

1 Moth
2 Hoodoo

StepArt T-shirts

•**DESIGN & ILLUSTRATION**
Bene Rohlmann
•**CLIENT**
StepArt
•**PHOTOGRAPHY**
StepArt

T-shirt illustrations for the
French brand StepArt.

2

1

3

1 Boxing Tiger
2 Wonders of Life
3 Circus Paradise

Alessandra Not Approved Apparel Illustration

- **DESIGN & ILLUSTRATION**
  Giorgia Lancellotti
- **PHOTOGRAPHY**
  Giorgia Lancellotti
- **MODEL**
  Eita Nakamura

"Alessandra Not Approved" is a personal project. Giorgia Lancellotti was inspired by old illustrations for children, and realized the project using traditional and digital techniques. The two illustrations represent a rabbit and a bear mistreated despite their love and care for a girl named Alessandra. Even if the illustrations have a childish taste, the black color and the vintage effect give them a noir and ironic mood, suitable for cool guys.

© GIORGIA LANCELLOTTI

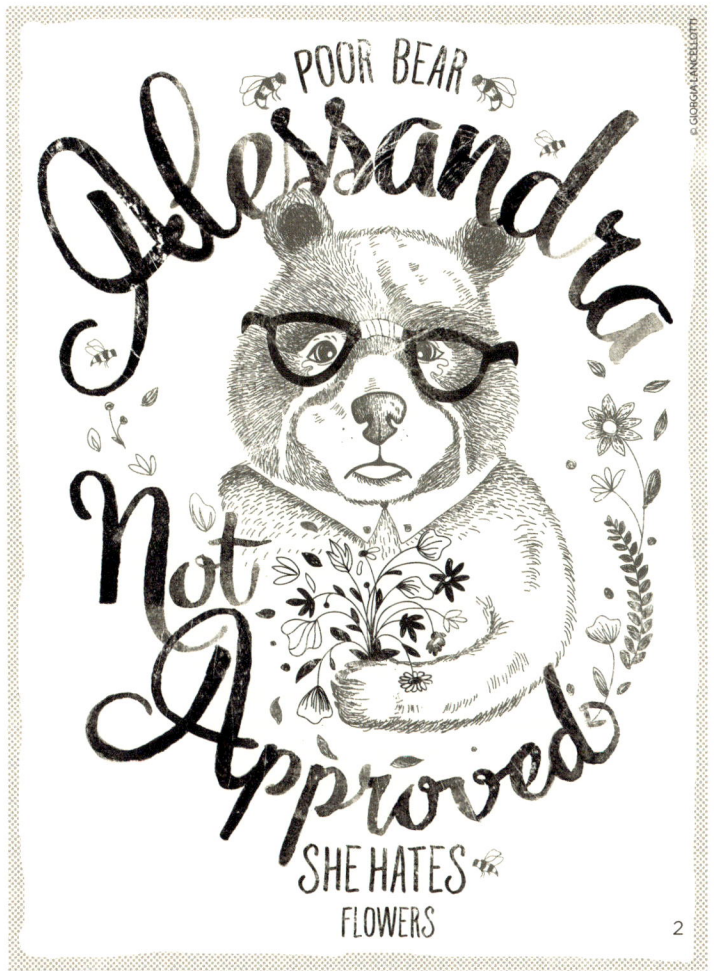

1 Poor Rabbit
2 Poor Bear

Nomad Face

•DESIGN & ILLUSTRATION
Igor Khrupin

Nomad Face is a personal streetwear brand by Igor Khrupin. It consists of a series of illustrations about travel and new discoveries.

Nike T-shirt Design

•DESIGN & ILLUSTRATION
Cristobal Ojeda (Newfren)
•CLIENT
Nike

Four T-shirt graphic designs for
Nike USA.

1   Alien
2   Free Run
3   Fear My Awesome
4   Nike Zone

Melody Soul
T-shirt Design

•**DESIGN & ILLUSTRATION**
Cristobal Ojeda (Newfren)

T-shirt graphic designs in two colors for Melody Soul
music production company from the U.S.A.

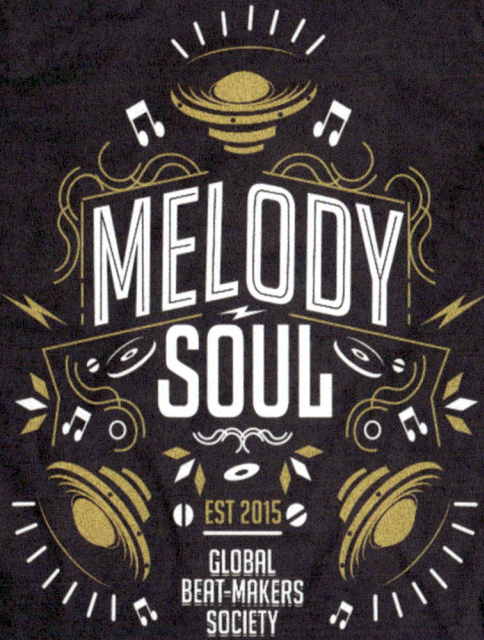

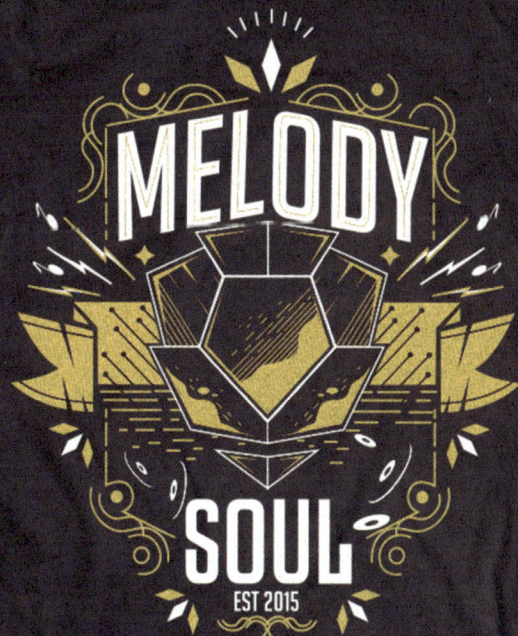

Devil's Advice for BlackMouth Co.

•**DESIGN & ILLUSTRATION**
Luiso Mostacho
•**CLIENT**
BlackMouth Co.
•**PHOTOGRAPHY**
Solecker

Devil's Advice is part of the 666 Collection from the brand BlackMouth Co. This screen-printed T-shirt signifies a turning point for the brand, bringing out the dark side of the soul.

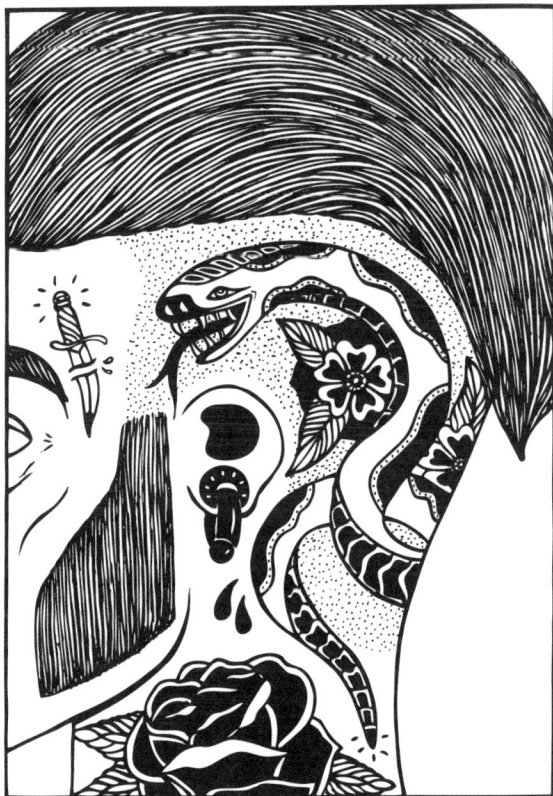

3rd Rail X
Tony Riff

•**DESIGN & ILLUSTRATION**
Tony Riff
•**CLIENT**
3rd Rail

A limited run of hand screen printed sticker packs and t-shirts created for UK based print studio 3rd Rail. The design made its debut at the London Illustration Fair and is currently available in their online store.

Words on Faces

•DESIGN & ILLUSTRATION
Olesya Bogoley

This project is devoted to world-renowned figures. Their words are forever imprinted on their faces, like powerful messages to descendants. All illustrations bear some sort of intimate message in which each viewer could find his or her own meaning. This is a project for people who enjoy reading between the lines, or tattoo lovers, or those who simply like good graphics. Be true, be brave, and stay young!

1 Anton Chekhov
2 Vladimir Mayakovsky
3 Fyodor Dostoyevsky
4 Alexander Pushkin
5 Ernest Hemingway

А. Чехов   1

Вл. Маяковский   2

Ф. Достоевский   3

А. Пушкин   4

Ernest Hemingway   5

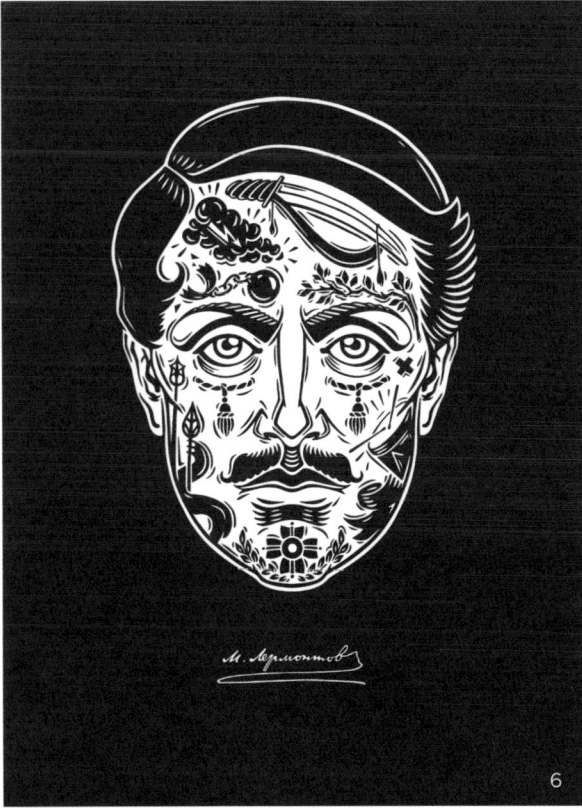

М. Лермонтовъ

6

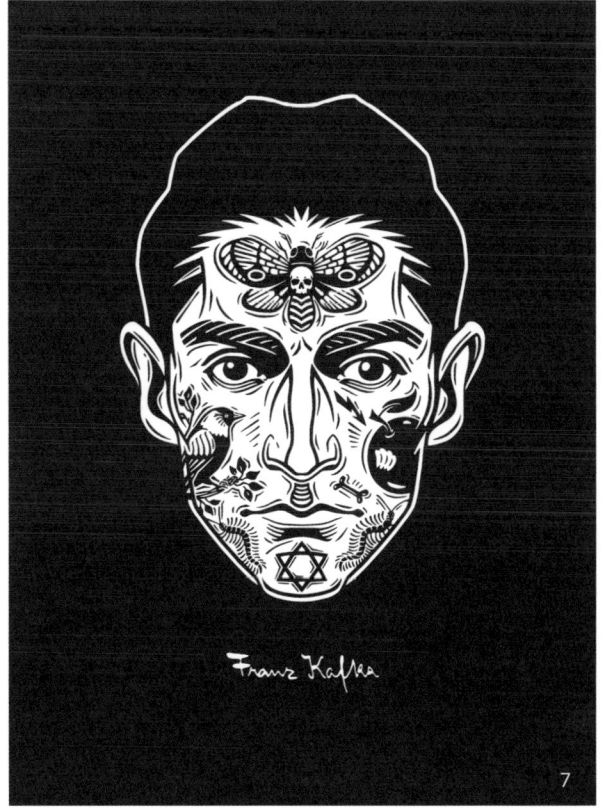

Franz Kafka

7

William Shakspere

8

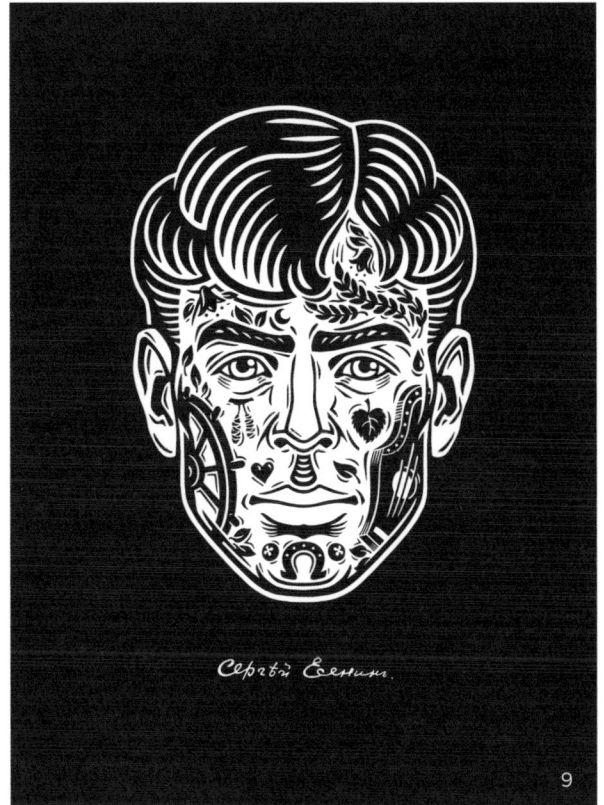

Сергѣй Есенинъ

9

6 Mikhail Lermontov
7 Franz Kafka
8 William Shakespeare
9 Sergei Yesenin

Syndicate Original

•DESIGN & ILLUSTRATION
Venya Son
•CLIENT
Syndicate Original

In collaboration with Syndicate Original, a Ukrainian streetwear brand, Venya Son designed a series of sharp illustrations for the brand's 2016 collection.

Save Your Money

•DESIGN & ILLUSTRATION
Mr. Kone

With the theme of money and the need for it, Mr. Kone thought up the idea of making a collection to play with the issue of money. They launched a collection full of characters and ideas about money.

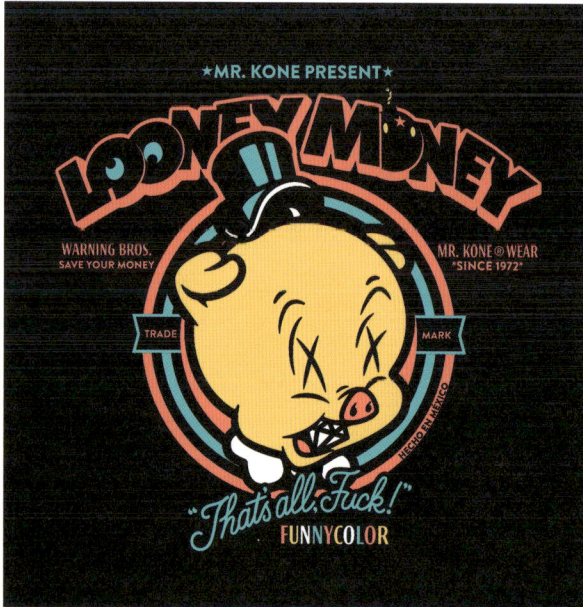

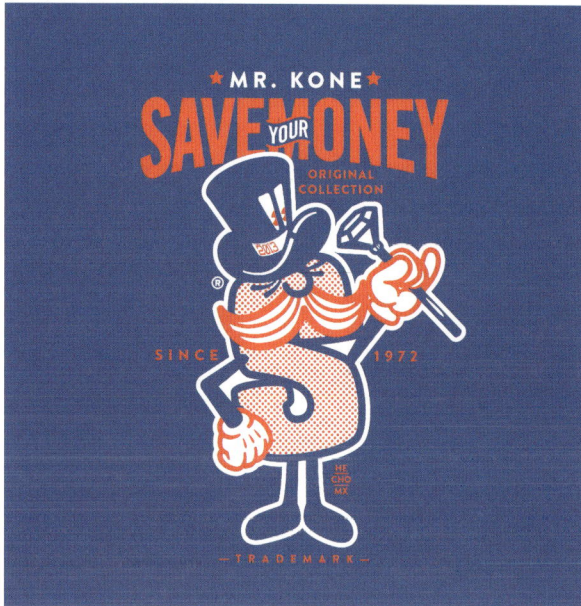

Fungolia T-shirt Design

•**DESIGN AGENCY**
 Dock 57
•**DESIGN & ILLUSTRATION**
 Sveta Shubina, Manar Shajri
•**ART DIRECTION**
 Calvin Tsoi, To Yu Fung
•**CLIENT**
 Fungolia
•**PHOTOGRAPHY**
 Calvin Tsoi, To Yu Fung

FUNGOLIA is a new independent lifestyle and apparel brand from Hong Kong, founded by Calvin Tsoi and Helen To, the legendary "Tokyo Walker," well known for her outrageous hosting style on her popular TV Travel programs. The core value of the brand closely parallels Helen's own lifestyle, which is to travel non-stop and to be full of fun. "Travel Animal" is a special line of T-shirts that inspires people to bring out the travel animal from within.

3

1

4

2

5

1 Bulldog
2 Guru Traveler
3 Hippie Traveler
4 Monkey
5 Yak

Hospital Use Only

•DESIGN & ILLUSTRATION
Petr Kudláček
•ART DIRECTION
Martin Míčka

From the beginning, the designers wanted to accent their love for fashion and music, to create something unique and special — something that would live and breathe with them. Hospital Use Only is based on their lives: on their incompetence to learn more than ten tricks in fourteen years, on their stupid sense of humor, or probably on something else. They do not really remember why they started this project and what it was for, but it was what they most wanted to create!

My Bones

•**DESIGN & ILLUSTRATION**
Natalia Pastukhova,
Alexey Ponomarchuk

An array of watercolor illustrations for T-shirts. The animal
themed illustrations are an ode to the season of winter.

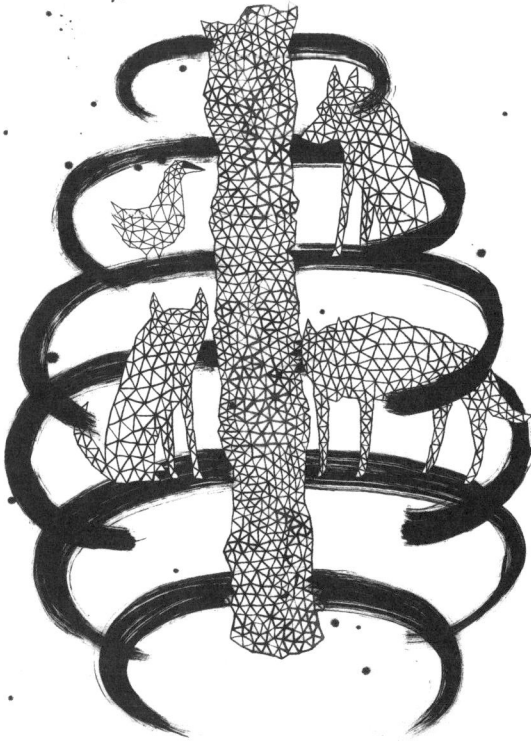

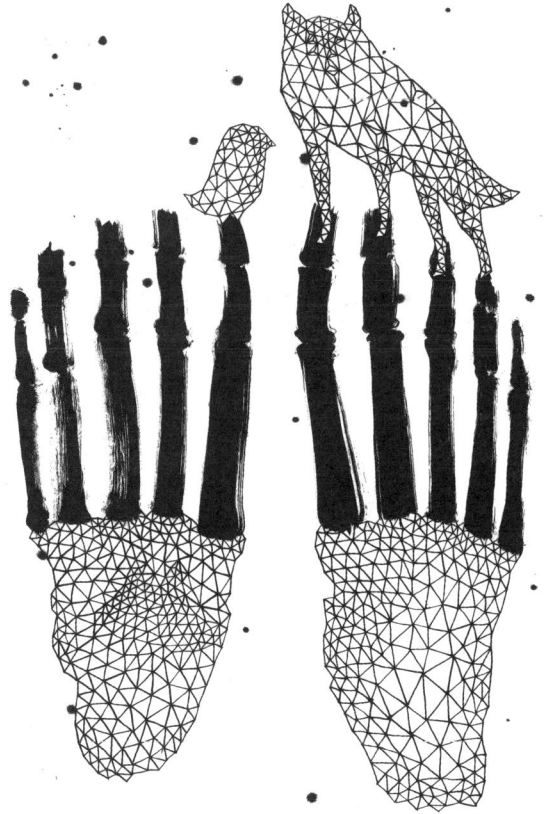

IGNAT'EV INK X WOLEE

- **DESIGN & ILLUSTRATION**
  Maxim Ignat'ev (IGNAT'EV INK)
- **CLIENT**
  WOLEE, OTDEL
- **PHOTOGRAPHY**
  WOLEE, Protasov Artem

Maxim Ignat'ev developed some illustrations for the street clothing brand WOLEE from St. Petersburg. The garments stood out with the prints of three Japanese traditional characters, namely the wolf, Godzilla, and death. The words "Master of Life" on the sleeves symbolize the human desire to be the master of one's life.

1 The Wolf for WOLEE
2 The Godzilla for WOLEE
3 The Death for WOLEE and OTDEL

1

2

3

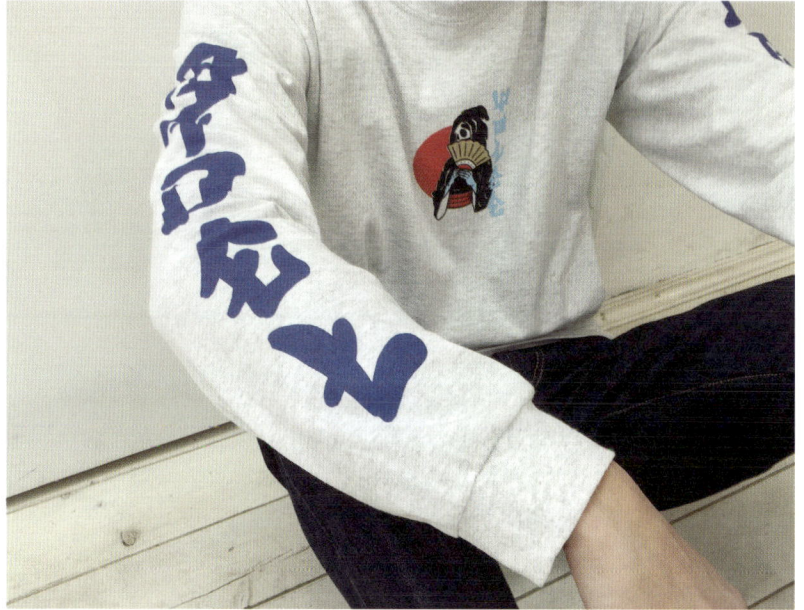

SOCKS & SHOES

Juan Díaz-Faes

Based in Madrid, Juan Díaz-Faes started working as an illustrator in 2011. He obtained his Bachelor of Fine Arts in 2005 and then a Doctorate on the Creative Process. His work tends to have a great graphic and narrative weight. He collaborates monthly with several magazines such as *MUWOM*, *Yorokobu*, and so on. He is part of the collective Ultrarradio, where new artists publish their work and spread the culture of drawing. He is also a professor of the One Year Course in Illustration at IED Visual Madrid.

INTERVIEW

– What originally drove you to become an illustrator?

I was always drawing since I was a child. I studied Fine Arts and then went for a PhD in Applied Creativity and Creative Process. Before working as an illustrator, I worked as a cameraman for a Spanish TV channel. At the same time, I was drawing and making some money for that. When I finally made enough money, I left the TV world and focused on drawing. I have now been working as a full-time illustrator for 7 years.

– How would you describe your design process? What materials do you enjoy working with the most?

I worked a lot for the press, so I used to draw very quickly and I loved the digital process, quick and clean. But now I came back to analog drawing. The smell of the materials and the fear of making mistakes motivate my painting and discovery of new techniques.

– How would you define your personal style?

I really love funny stuff and I am always laughing, so I bring some of these elements into my work. Maybe I have a funny and hilarious style (I don't know). I love the style of Horror Vacui, so in most of my work I try to fill in all the space and try not to leave any margins. Also, I think my style is clean because I usually work quickly, and I use no more than 3 or 4 colors.

– Your patterns have many cute characters. Where do you usually get inspiration?

I like imagining a story and letting the characters appear naturally. Generally, I just know that one or two things

are the "must have" in my pattern, while the rest are just elements which keep appearing as I draw. When drawing a pattern, I enjoy introducing some funny bonuses that viewers will discover only if they spend some time looking.

– What would you consider to be your proudest achievement so far in your design career?

My best achievement is that I can make a live drawing. Just like I said before, I am coming back to analog painting, so everyday when I start working on a live-drawing, I always think about how lucky I am. I have recently finished painting 25 skateboards for a solo exhibition.

– Do you have any advice for illustrators who aspire to design their own pattern?

Here is my advice (I think it suits other occupations as well): be funny, work a lot, study the works you like and dislike, and try to discover your own way of making patterns.

– What else are you keen on besides design?

Draw, eat, and laugh equally! So besides design, I like food, music, and laughter.

– What is your motto?

My motto is: Díaz-Faes draws, eats, and laughs equally, and if he stops doing stuff, he gets bored.

Pattern Socks

•**DESIGN & ILLUSTRATION**
  Juan Díaz-Faes
•**CLIENT**
  Parachanclas
•**PHOTOGRAPHY**
  Parachanclas

Juan Díaz-Faes designed a
collection of patterns for socks.

1 Postparty
2 Noche

PARACHANCLAS!
socks designed and made in Barcelona
BY DIAZ FAES

Pacific and Co. Socks

•DESIGN & ILLUSTRATION
Marcos Navarro
•STYLIST
Ana Sting
•MAKE UP
Itziar Llorente
•MODEL
Camilo Ramirez
•PHOTOGRAPHY
Laia Benavides

Marcos Navarro designed two all-over prints, Monkey Gang and Sea Soul, in collaboration with Pacific and Co., a Spanish socks brand with a unique style based in Barcelona.

1 Monkey Gang
2 Sea Soul

Bnomio X Pacific and Co.

•**DESIGN & ILLUSTRATION**
Bnomio
•**ART DIRECTION**
Bnomio
•**PHOTOGRAPHY**
Juanma Jmse
•**CLIENT**
Pacific and Co.

Pacific and Co. Pharaoh socks is the collaboration between Pacific and Co. and the artist Bnomio, which is also part of Bnomio's Egypt Tattoo Flash collection.

Space and Hedgehog Socks

•**DESIGN & ILLUSTRATION**
Jagoda Jankowska
•**CLIENT**
Many Mornings
•**PHTOGRAPHY**
Maciej Butkowski

The Space and Hedgehog patterns were made for the autumn collection of Many Mornings, a Polish socks brand. The socks are one-size-fits-all, unisex, and for both adults and kids, so the target is to make everyone smile when seeing and wearing these socks. The patterns are made of a limited amount of pixels and colors. During the creative process, the designer had to focus on making the illustrations universal and, most of all, cheerful.

1 Space
2 Hedgehog

2

Sammy Icon Socks

- **DESIGN & ILLUSTRATION**
  Anton Abo
- **CLIENT**
  Sammy Icon
- **PHOTOGRAPHY**
  8calibr

A series of line illustrations and colorful pattern design for Sammy Icon socks.

1 Radier
2 Aragon
3 Jaune
4 Hunker
5 Furphy

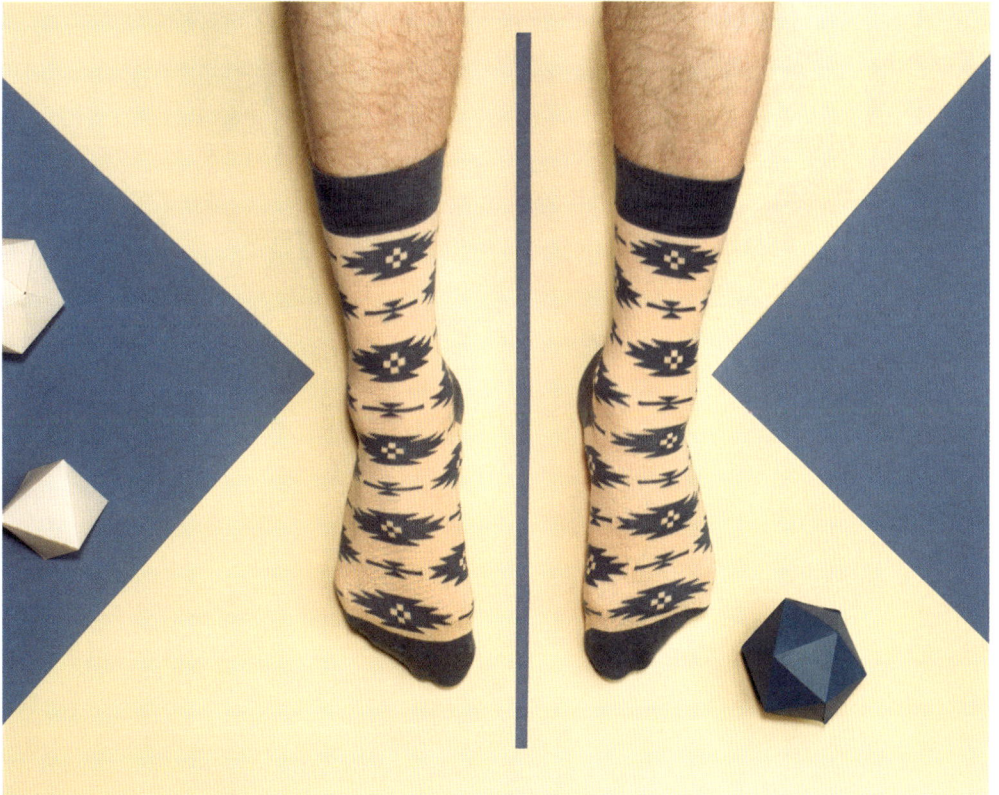

GOT NOTHING ELSE TO DO!
I'm on a high.
STREET AWESOME
BEAM ME UP!
EAT!
DOODLE!
RAWR!
sushi!
oops.
slip!
burn!
AH!
BOX O' MAGIC!
YEAH!
RIP

Lei Melendres

Lei Melendres is an illustrator and professional doodle artist whose works have been featured in different esteemed publications as well as local and international galleries and exhibitions. Lei enjoys creating the intensity of endless details and elements that interact together to form a scene. His doodle art is defined by repetition, patterns, monsters, animals, unimaginable creatures, the unknown, and other weird stuff.

INTERVIEW

– What originally drove you to become an illustrator and doodler?

I started drawing at a very young age and it has become a hobby of mine ever since. As a teenager, I have always wanted to have a job wherein I would be able to use my skills or at least be able to draw. I have never expected that I would be doing it as a full time job.

Over the years, I have tried many types and styles of drawing with the goal of being able to draw anything as I please. I have put in many hours of practice every day just to satisfy myself with the output. In the end, I never mastered any of the styles but "doodle art." I was able to make use of all the lessons I learned and I managed to combine them to create my own style of art.

– How would you describe your design process?

My process differs for every purpose that my art is intended. Some clients would prefer that I send a sketch of the artwork before I get into inking it. That means I have to commit to the process of planning each and every element to use. Sometimes, I even ask other clients to make a list of all the elements they want to include in the artwork. For some, they let me do whatever I want. The latter is what I prefer. Spontaneous and on the spot.

– How would you define your personal style?

A personal style is your signature as an artist. My personal style consists of how I create an interactive mix of elements to form a scene with a bit of story. I call it "Infinity Mix."

– The doodled shoes you created show many detailed characters. Where do you usually get inspiration?

I love character design. I enjoy it so much that I challenge myself to come up with as many unique characters as I can without repeating by making different combinations and inventing new ways. I get my inspiration from almost anything around me. Artworks by other artists and even normal objects scattered all around me are enough to inspire me to create something new. When I look at an object, I sometimes imagine it as a living thing who has a face, some limbs, and a personality.

– For you, what is the hardest part when doodling directly on the surface of shoes and other articles?

The hardest part for me would be the process of trial and error on what materials to use on my chosen surface. There is always a perfect material for every surface and the truth is, you really have to put a lot of time in learning what to use and how to use them. I tried 6 pens before I was able to choose the pen that worked best with the Adidas Classic Superstar.

– In your opinion, what role does graphic design and illustration play in streetwear, like apparel, shoes, socks, headwear, etc.?

I think lately, people have been attracted to apparel with a little bit of illustration and creativity drawn or sewn on it. In the past, brands would downright write their brand names on their products as big as they could without a touch of subtlety and people would buy it. Jackets would have large drawings and many different creative art patches just to make it look more personal or flashy. Socks and shoes are now works of art with different artworks and many colors. I think this is proof that people are slowly making art into something mainstream.

– What would you consider to be your proudest achievement so far in your design career?

I am the head of the biggest active doodling community in the Philippines named "Doodle Art Enthusiasts." I treat their success as something I am proud of because a lot of the members look up to me and would share how much I inspired them to become better artists. With the growing community of artists, the competitiveness of art making is through the roof, and to still be able to make a living with my hobby is already something I consider as an achievement.

– Do you have any advice for illustrators who aspire to enter the world of streetwear?

If you are really into illustration and art in general, I would suggest you try using different mediums as a canvas for your art. You will really learn a lot from the experience and should also try to enjoy the experimental stage as much as you can. Asking advice from other artists who are already doing it helps a lot, but nothing beats trying everything out for yourself.

– What else are you keen on besides design?

I love music almost as much as I love visual arts. When I am not making art, I really enjoy cooking and watching movies.

– What is your motto?

Do your best today. Do better tomorrow.

Doodle Superstar: Classic Black Stripes & Inverted White Stripes

- **DESIGN & ILLUSTRATION**
  Lei Melendres
- **CLIENT**
  Kim Gabriel
- **PHOTOGRAPHY**
  Lei Melendres

Lei Melendres created a personal art series entitled "Doodle Shoes" in which he doodled on several different brands of shoes. The Classic Black Stripes project took the Adidas Superstar model and added a twist of having doodle elements as the stripes, instead of the usual black color fill. The white area featured less doodles to show the contrast between the black and the white areas.

The idea behind the Inverted White Stripes project was to have super detailed doodles on the shoes while leaving the stripes clean. The contrast between the two areas would make the stripes the center of attention from afar, while on a closer look the doodled area would shine as well.

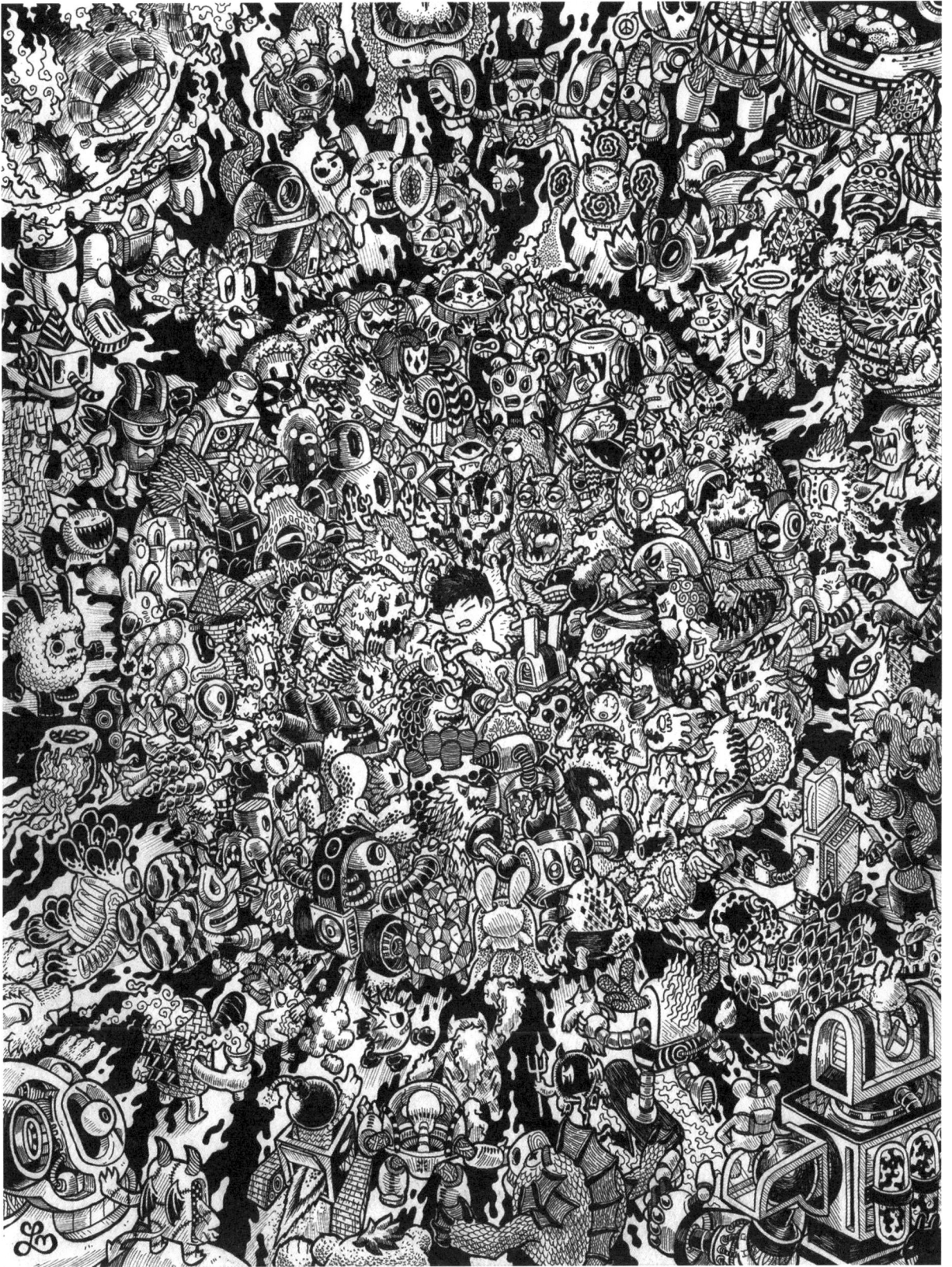

Caccia Grossa

- **DESIGN AGENCY**
  Isoì
- **DESIGN & ART DIRECTION**
  Daniele Desperati
- **ILLUSTRATION & CRAFT**
  Gaia Bernasconi

Caccia Grossa is an original design project created by Isoì in 2015, which involves illustrations, screenprints, engravings, embroidery, and handpainted shoes.

MC Gey X VANS

•**DESIGN & ILLUSTRATION**
Jakub Rafael
•**CLIENT**
VANS, Ty Nikdy Label
•**PHOTOGRAPHY**
Katarina Bell

This is a special limited illustrated edition of VANS shoes. It is a project in collaboration with the music artist MC Gey from the label Ty Nikdy and the company VANS for charity purposes.

Arrels Shoes

•**DESIGN & ILLUSTRATION**
Catalina Estrada
•**ART DIRECTION**
Hey
•**PHOTOGRAPHY**
Roc Canals, Adoni Beristain
•**CLIENT**
Arrels Shoes

Commissioned by Arrels Shoes, Catalina Estrada created three patterns for the brand's shoes — two for women and one for men. In the design, Catalina wanted to go back to the tropical jungle because she finds it exotic and powerful in equal measure. She wanted to evoke the jungle with memories of scenes that she had seen in Colombia, combining dreams with reality.

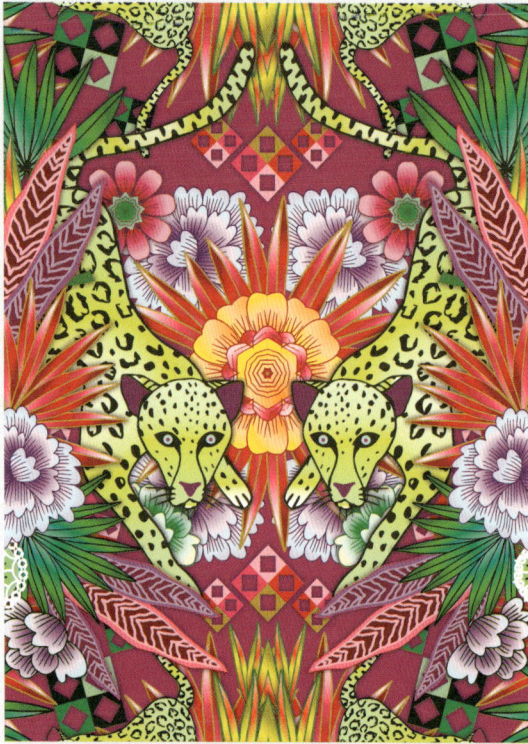

Design on Shoes

•DESIGN & ILLUSTRATION
Pamela Gallegos

Pamela Gallegos hand-painted two Bucketfeet shoes with pencils and acrylic paints. The pattern and illustration are inspired by the designer's Peruvian roots. The shapes and colors stand for her beautiful culture.

▲ PeruNative
▼ Paititi

Sneakers for Rew

- **ILLUSTRATION**
  Gabriele Bonavera
- **DESIGN**
  Vans
- **Photography**
  Gabriele Bonavera

Gabriele Bonavera hand-drew these Vans shoes for Italian artist Rew. The inspiration for this drawing came from hip hop music.

Arrels X Raül

•**DESIGN**
  Raül Garcia Gili
•**CLIENT**
  Arrels Barcelona

Arrels, which means "roots" in Catalan, is a Barcelona based footwear brand for the urban market. The blend of optimism, color, and rhythm defines the slogan of the company: Upbeat shoes. The shoes are based on a sound experiment that the designer carried out in Barcelona. He recorded sounds in different parts of the city, processed them graphically, and then created the print using that graphic representation. From this, people can talk about different Barcelona neighborhoods, streets or emblematic spots — La Barceloneta, La Diagonal or the Collserola Tower — in a very unique way, that is, through its sounds.

BARCELONETA   DIAGONAL   TORRE COLLSEROLA

Pattern for Bucketfeet

•**DESIGN & ILLUSTRATION**
  Kevin Bongang
•**CLIENT**
  Bucketfeet

Kevin Bongang created two original pattern designs for Bucketfeet shoes. The patterns are made of daily random things like burgers, French fries, coke and so on, reflecting the casual urban brand.

Havaianas Flip Flops

•DESIGN & ILLUSTRATION
Mario Carpe
•CLIENT
Havaianas

An illustration of an island is printed on the inner sole of the flip flops. When customers walk with their Havaianas flip flops, they will feel the island in every step they take.

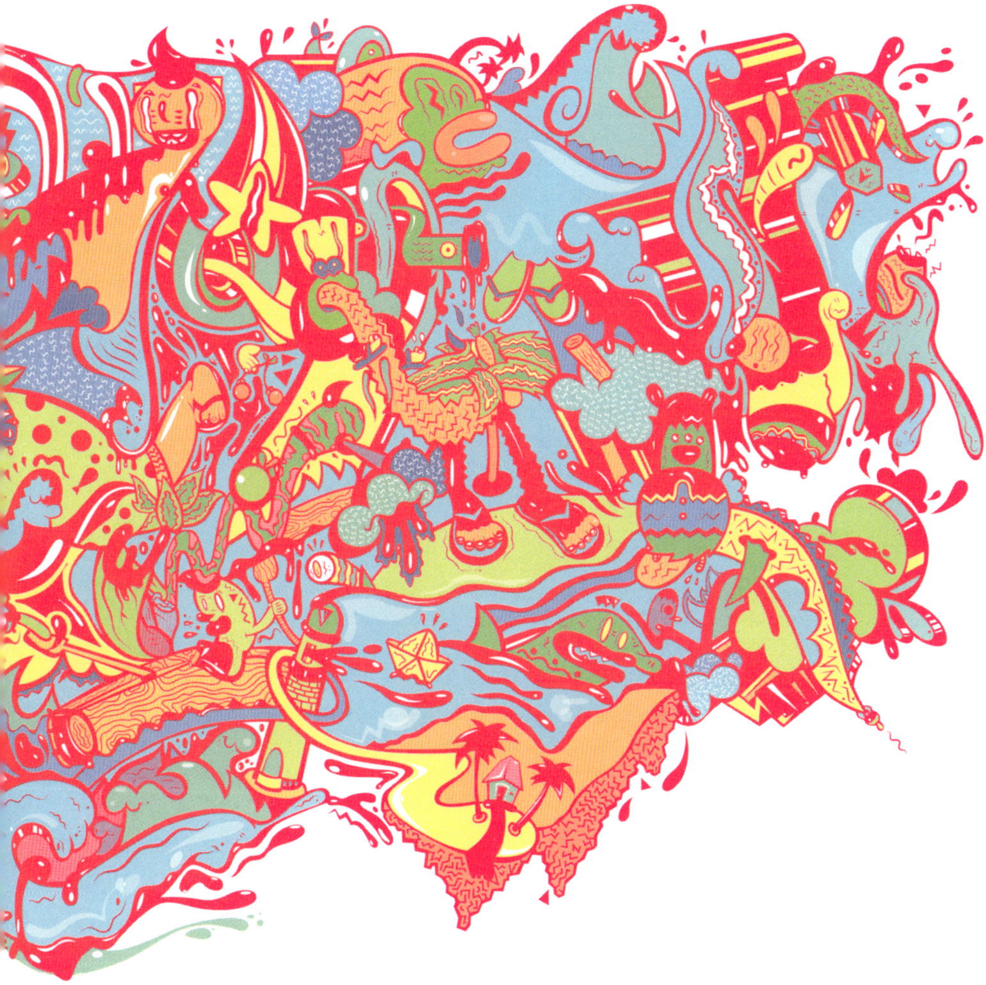

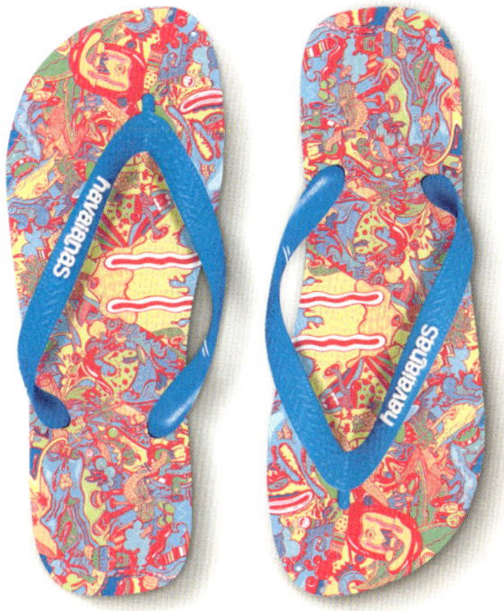
havaianas
havaianas

80's California Vans Shoes: Local Lover

•**DESIGN**
Keiji Ishida
•**PHOTOGRAPHY**
Shinji Ishida

The shoes are based on the theme of 80's California, combining patterns that reflect local California surroundings and skate culture.

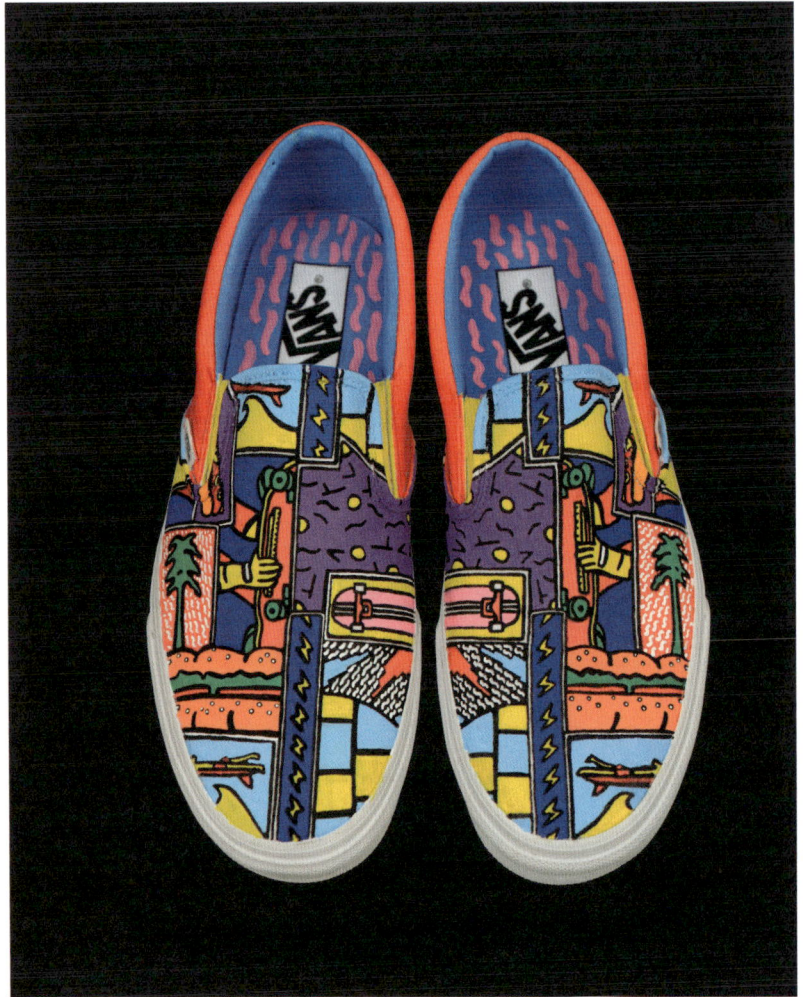

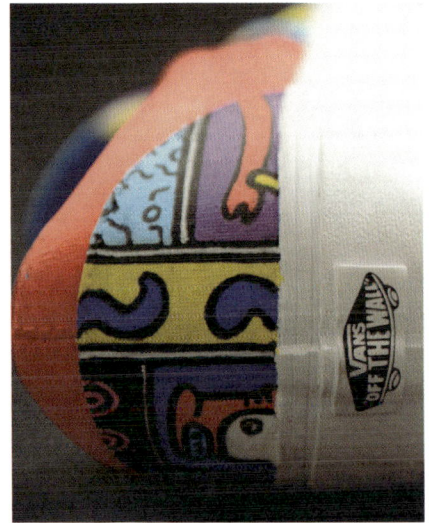

ACCESSORIES

THE RIGHT CHOICE IS WITHING
YOUR

MY WAY ♡

WE ARE
WHAT WE REPEATEDLY DO
ARISTOTLE

Catherine Stepanishcheva

Catherine Stepanishcheva is a textile designer and illustrator based in Ukraine. She is passionate about textile design and her dream is to create her own clothing fabric, which is gradually becoming reality.

INTERVIEW

– What originally drove you to become an illustrator and textile designer?

Since I was a kid, I loved drawing and working with clay. At that time, my only dream was to become an artist. At the age of 13, I learned about batik, which is a kind of painting on silk. This led to the fact that I eventually chose textile trends as my profession. By the time I went to the university, there was a very interesting course — textile design. From then on, I realized that I wanted to create fabric with my own patterns. It is an incredible pleasure for me to see someone use the fabric with my own patterns and illustrations!

– How do you define your project "My Silk Story"? Please share with us the story behind it.

Before starting the project My Silk Story, I made designs for my own postcards and notebooks. I also developed designs of linen table cloth for a Ukrainian company. But I never forgot my desire to create my own textiles, so I started the project My Silk Story. This project is very special for me because all my thoughts, feelings, and sensations are embodied in one piece of gentle silk. When touching the silk, people know that there is another universe in this piece of thin, weightless, and soft world of unveiled secrets and mysteries. In this project, I am always looking for new interesting forms and ideas, and I am not afraid to approach any topic that excites me. I think I am realizing my dream with My Silk Story.

– How would you describe your design approach?

My creative process primarily consists of my thoughts. It is very important for me to express in my work my own inner world, and to put in the creation the sense and message that I want to communicate to the world. Before starting a project, I think about the colors that can best display my mood. Then I draw some sketches or immediately embark on the main work.

I like to mix techniques and materials. I often paint with watercolors, then I scan the images and modify it in the computer to create a layout for printing. Recently I got carried away with line drawings — they are very crisp and graphic.

– How would you describe your personal style?

Bright and optimistic. In my work, I try not to use depressive or aggressive themes, because I think we have enough of such phenomena in our lives. I believe that the aim of my work is inviting people to the light side of life.

– The backdrop of your project "Dialogue" is very intriguing and inspiring. Where do you get inspiration?

It is one of my favorite projects! The idea came spontaneously. I usually like keeping all things in order and under control, while this project helped me let go of the situation and accept things as they are. I collected participants' answers to questions and drew the things their answers brought to mind. The idea of this project is to put myself in an improvisational mode and I think that improvisation makes us a little bit better.

– Do you consider yourself trendy? How would you interpret urban fashion?

I never chase the latest fashion trends, but I always try to dress myself with some zest. It can be beautiful colors, interesting accessories, and unusual design — I cannot get enough of the clothes with unusual textile patterns.

Urban fashion is the fashion of individuality. I think people choose and wear the clothing that reflects their inner world and feelings, which helps them stand out from the crowd.

– Do you have any advice for illustrators who aspire to enter the world of textile design?

I think the key thing in textile design is to stay original and do unusual patterns which are fun to look at for a long time. Designers should be honest with people in the themes they choose.

– What else are you keen on besides design and your work?

I cannot imagine my life without music! Recently I started to collect children's books with interesting illustrations and postage stamps. I also try my hand at calligraphy. It is very interesting and meditative, which helps me learn a lot about myself.

My Silk Story:
Universe Collection

•**DESIGN & ILLUSTRATION**
Catherine Stepanishcheva
•**PHOTOGRAPHY**
Yana Godenko
•**MODEL**
Mira Rismyatova

The Universe Collection is designed for 2017, which is considered to be the year of fiery Rooster. The project began with the idea of an egg, or rather the thought of its perfection and uniqueness. Roosters inside eggs symbolize the divine essence that is responsible for the creative ability that exists in every human being. Under the influence of this thought, the essence moves on to action — this is the process of creating something new and unknown.

My Silk Story:
Silk Scarves Dialogue

•**DESIGN & ILLUSTRATION**
Catherine Stepanishcheva
•**PHOTOGRAPHY**
Yana Godenko
•**MODEL**
Mira Rismyatova

The collection Dialogue began with a question of Catherine's interest: "What is happiness for you?" She started a project online in which people could give their own answer. Catherine chose the answers that she really liked — "To love and be loved," which was given by one of the participants named Valeriia. After that, Catherine illustrated her question and Valeriia's answer. The next question was asked by Valeriia in a call-and-response fashion, until the entire plane of the first scarf was filled.

For the second scarf, the basic question was a short, but very comprehensive question from another participant Konstantine: "Who are we?" Again, all interested people could express their views. In this case, she illustrated all the answers on the scarf.

▲ What Is Happiness For You?
▼ Who Are We?

WHO ARE WE? (KONSTANTINE)

SOME

My Silk Story:
Silk Scarves Interaction

•**DESIGN & ILLUSTRATION**
 Catherine Stepanishcheva
•**PHOTOGRAPHY**
 Yana Godenko
•**MODEL**
 Sasha Godenko

Silk Scarves Interaction is a story about love and understanding. Catherine Stepanishcheva wishes that all people learn to hear and feel nature, to be close to it, and be a part of it. Mammals, birds, plants and insects on the scarves are not selected randomly. All the characters of this story are included in the *Red Book of Ukraine,* a list of endangered animal and plants living in Ukraine. They are a confirmation and a reminder of what can happen if human beings do not learn to appreciate nature and live in harmony with it. By being a single entity, people can truly be happy. Phrases in Latin, which are located on the perimeter of the scarves, emphasize the concept of the collection.

Scarves for Jopo

•ILLUSTRATION
Sofia Noceti
•CLIENT
Jopo

Flat illustrations in whimsical
color palettes on scarves for
Jopo Wearable Textile Design.
It is clear that nature has been
and still is Sofia's chosen muse,
as draped scarves are elegantly
adorned with vibrant foliage.

Maew-Nalisa Scarf

- **DESIGN & ILLUSTRATION**
  Tikkywow
- **CLIENT**
  Handicapped Animals Foundation
- **PHOTOGRAPHY**
  Tikkywow

This project comes from the intention of helping homeless animals, especially disabled or handicapped cats. By combining the beauty of art that people would enjoy with the image of a cat, the designer came up with the pattern for the Maew-Nalisa scarf. "Maew-Nalisa" means "Monalisa + Cat", as "meaw" means "cat" in Thai. A range of colors are mixed to make the scarf shiny and fun.

ARTIFICIO

•DESIGN & ILLUSTRATION
Cee Neira
•ART DIRECTION
Artificio
•PHOTOGRAPHY
Charly Toledo

ARTIFICIO is a silk scarves project focused on creating original patterns to print on textile. Its inspiration comes from sketching, illustration, and collage. With the patterns, the designers want to catch the attention of people who like artsy styles and want to add visual and graphic elements to their outfits. This fashion brand is from Argentina and aspires towards global recognition.

1 Pop
2 Veleros

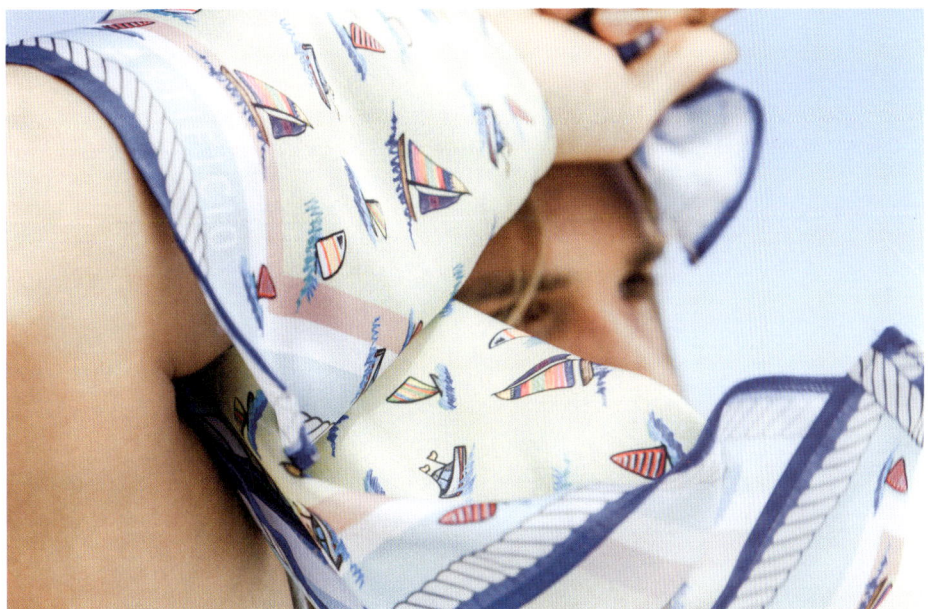

Why Duck Brand

•**DESIGN & ILLUSTRATON**
 Why Duck
•**PHOTOGRAPHY**
 Sebastian Ścigalski, Dawid Ścigalski

Why Duck created a set of
headwear graphics for their
own clothing brand Why Duck.

1 & 2 Tiger

1

2

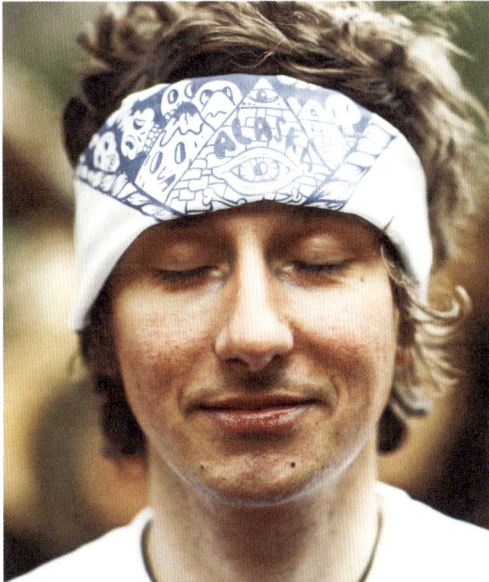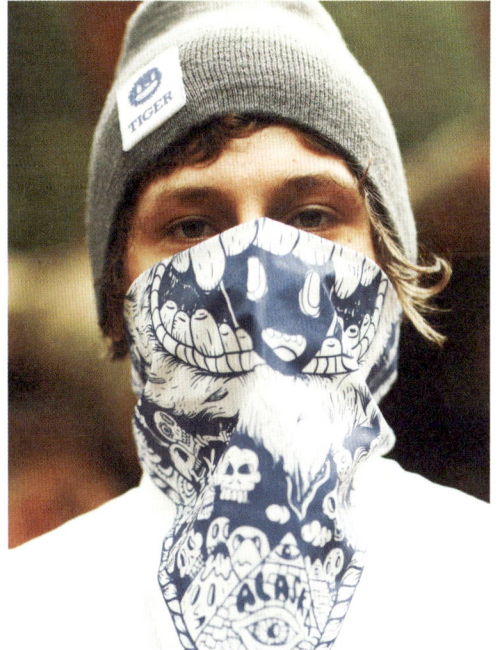

Slash Snowboards Neck Warmer

•**DESIGN & ILLUSTRATION**
  Michael Hacker
•**ART DIRECTION**
  David Fernandez, Gigi Rüf
•**CLIENT**
  Slash Snowboards

Michael Hacker designed three different monster faces for Slash Snowboards which were applied to the brand's neck warmer. Customers can wear this neck warmer in three different ways depending on their current mood.

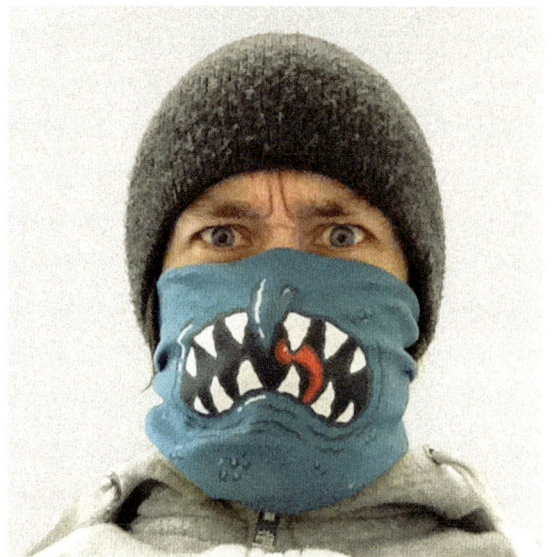

Kiki's Cocoa:
Halloween Edition

- **DESIGN & ILLUSTRATION**
  Chi Michalski (ChiChiLand)
- **MODEL**
  Mycho Cocoa
- **CLIENT**
  Kiki's Cocoa

Collaborating with Kiki's Cocoa, Chi Michalski designed and hand-printed a series of Halloween-themed bandanas. Inspired by furoshiki, the Japanese art of cloth wrapping, the fabrics served a double function: for clothing and for packaging, exclusively for Kiki's Chocolate Club members. The characters were laser-cut from linoleum blocks and then hand stamped (block printed) onto black cotton fabric. Inspired in equal part by traditional Day of the Dead imagery as well as contemporary character designs, these unique bandanas were only produced in a limited run, making for a wonderful Halloween surprise for their recipients.

Tote Bags: Trend +
My, Your, Our Story

•**DESIGN & ILLUSTRATION**
Helen Borg
•**CREATIVE DIRECTION**
Marlene Wasserman
•**MOCK UP**
GraphicBurger

Helen Borg was asked to design imagery for a selection of tote bags in light of current design trends. She looked to society for conceptual inspiration and created a series of cheeky imagery in relation to people's needs, wants, and desires. Her designs are targeted at the contemporary female buyer who is not afraid to make a bold statement.

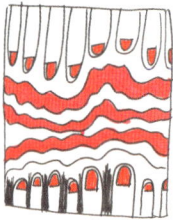

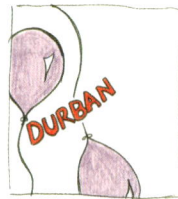

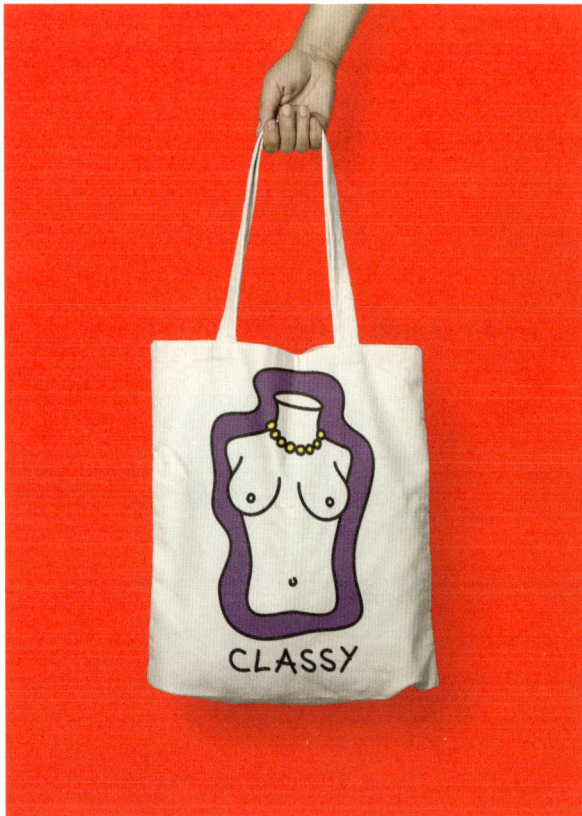

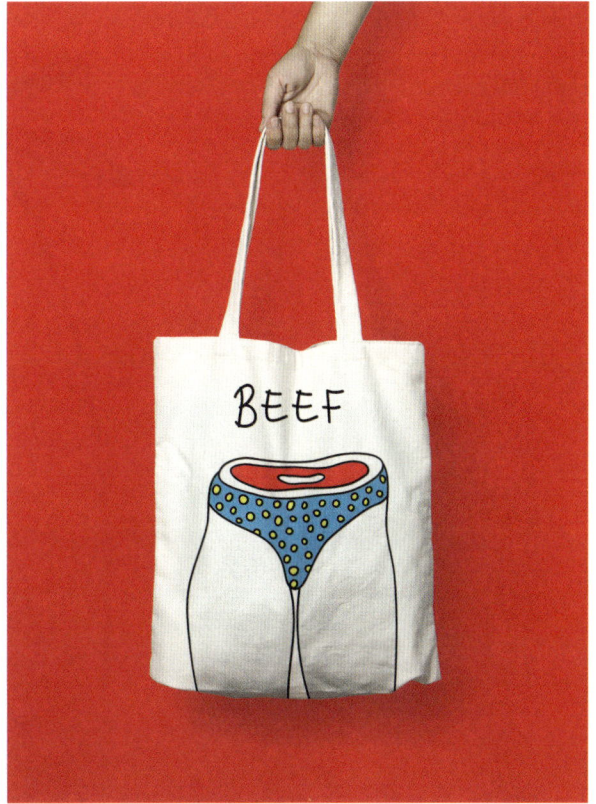

Girls Just Wanna Have Fun

•DESIGN & ILLUSTRATION
Verónica de Arriba (Depeapa)
•PHOTOGRAPHY
Argider Aparicio

Girls Just Wanna Have Fun is a
collection of 100% cotton tote
bags. The bags are screen-
printed with line illustrations
of three girls who just want to
have fun.

YOU ARE CUTE
by depeapa

YOU ARE AMAZING
by depeapa

YOU ARE AWESOME
by depeapa

Custom Tote Bags

•DESIGN & ILLUSTRATION
Ana Costov

A couple of interesting illustrations for custom tote bags designed by Ana Costov, an illustrator from Republic of Moldova. In her work, she portraits her desire to wander through the whole world. Sometimes she creates worlds and places with faces that she has seen or probably would never see.

1 Friends
2 Glamorous
3 Morning Ride
4 The Bicycle

1

2

3

4

Éram 90 ans

•DESIGN & ILLUSTRATION
The Feebles
•CLIENT
Éram

For the 90th anniversary of the brand Éram, The Feebles was invited to design a tote bag that captured the special moments and historic iconography of the brand. The tote bags are available in all Éram shops.

I Kill You

•DESIGN & ILLUSTRATION
Why Duck
•PHOTOGRAPHY
Sebastian Ścigalski

The project, I Kill You, was designed for the digital artists collective, Goverdose. The team has released only one e-zine in the past, however their friendship and passion for creating has never died. The illustration has been implemented as the print for a tote bag.

Tote Bag Collection

•DESIGN & ILLUSTRATION
The Red Wolf

The Red Wolf seeks to create illustrations with personality which reflect a modern lifestyle and elevate the female figure. Strong lines and colors are the elements that best represent their works. In this collection, "woman" and "nature" are two of the biggest inspirations for them. They believe that the starting point for creative work lies in a single moment of looking at something interesting, directing one's attention to color, shape, and figure.

1

1 Woman Rider
2 Yellow Bike
3 Woman Color

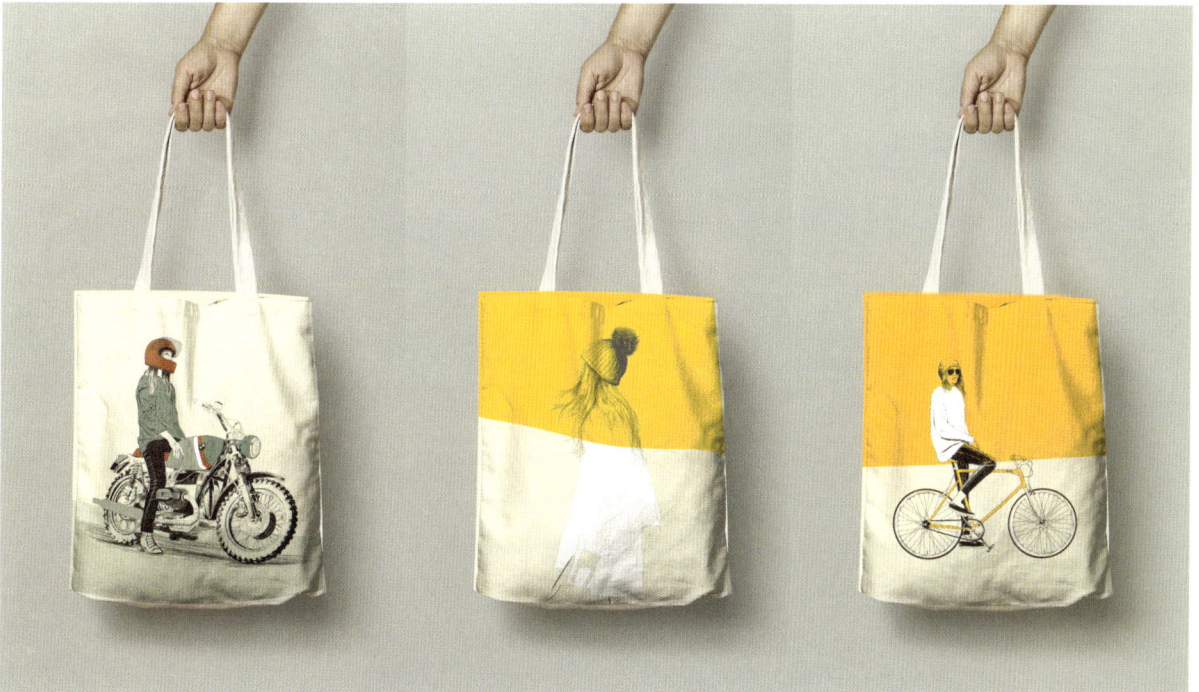

This is an illustration inspired by life on the streets of Prague, Czech Republic. It is printed on tote bags for Myokard project, launched by Dana Ledl.

Bread Bag for Lagarde

- **DESIGN & ILLUSTRATION**
  Monika Yaneva
- **MOCK UP**
  GraphicBurger
- **CLIENT**
  Lagarde Bulgaria
- **PHOTOGRAPHY**
  Monika Yaneva

Lagarde is the first and only factory in Bulgaria to produce French style bread. The bread bag was commissioned for their café chain "Café Olé" in Varna. The quirky illustrations celebrate the French traditions and lifestyle that the brand represents, while at the same time carrying a sense of humor and youthfulness. The designs contain symbols that illustrate French culture and a range of sweets and breads that the cafes offer.

Filter017 Razzle Dazzle Snapback Cap

- **DESIGN AGENCY**
  Filter017
- **DESIGN & ILLUSTRATION**
  Filter017
- **PHOTOGRAPHY**
  Filter017

This time Filter017 presents their classic pattern snapback cap collection. There are three pattens: The Pop Corn Gang, the Colorful pattern, their most popular pattern, and the Pop Patch pattern. These patterns are combined with a cap brim in a solid color.

1 Colorful Pattern
2 Pop Corn Gang
3 Pop Patch Pattern

OLD STYLE
Viva!
Retro Popularity
FRESH
FILTER 017
The Pop Corn Gang
BLING BLING
Butter
POP CORN
yum-yum!
FILTER017 Graphic Design
Not popcorn
POP!
Join us!
2

EST.2004
POP CORN GANG
MIXED SAUCE
Easy
GOOD RIVER
NEVER GIVE UP!!!
FUN IDEA
CREALIVE DEPT.
BRAINSTORMING
Popular
Funky Maker POP
DOCTOR WAY
FILTER017
TAXI CO.
MixedSauce & WonderWork
3

AMAZING
ORIGINALITY
MIXED SAUCE
Easy
Funky Maker

Filter017 Snapback Caps and Bucket Hats

•**DESIGN AGENCY**
Filter017
•**DESIGN & ILLUSTRATION**
Filter017
•**PHOTOGRAPHY**
Filter017

A collection of Filter017's caps and hats. The full outdoor graphics pattern is applied to both snapback caps and bucket hats. Cotton fabric, exquisite dying, and printing technology are used to increase the whole detail of the graphic pattern.

Pioneer snapback caps feature the Filter017's original "lost camouflage" pattern. Excellent suede fabric is used as the key splicing material.

1   Outdoor Graphics Pattern
2   Pioneer Snapback Cap

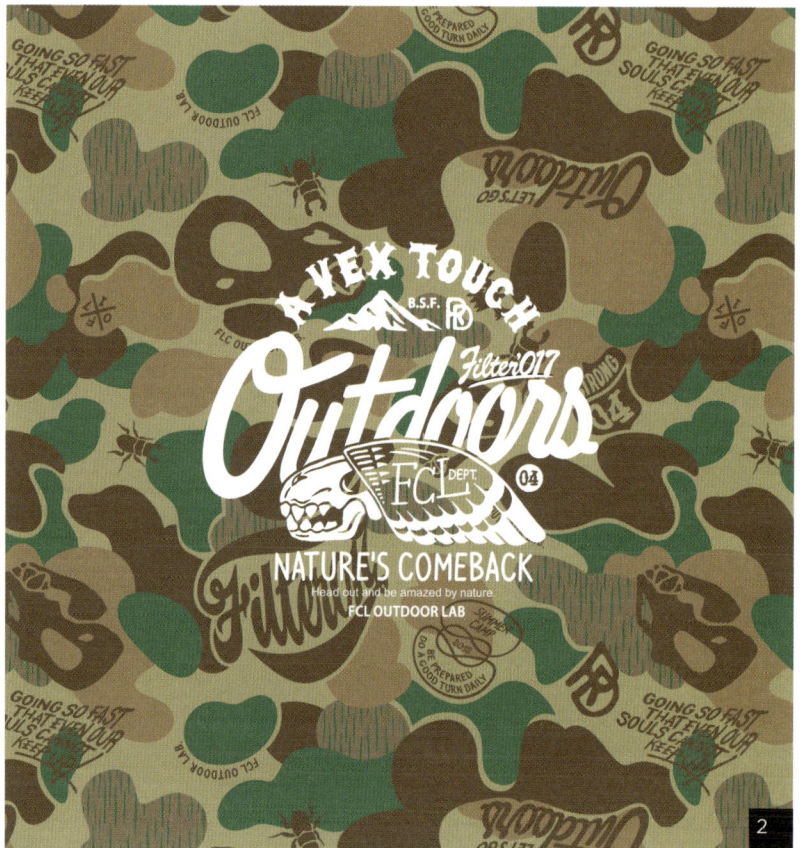

Historias de Cabeza

•**DESIGN & ILLUSTRATION**
Jairo Díaz Herrera
•**CLIENT**
Vector Cali

This project was based on conceptualizing thoughts of everyday life on the caps for the brand, Vector Cali.

Hats Galore

•**DESIGN & ILLUSTRATION**
Leanna Perry

An array of men's baseball, camper, bucket, and beanie hats featuring illustrated patterns by Leanna Perry. These hats are distributed in assorted retail stores across the globe including Forever 21, Urban Outfitters, Hot Topic, Target, Walmart, and Spencer's.

INDEX

123KLAN

www.123klan.com

Originally from France, 123KLAN was founded by husband and wife Scien and Klor in 1992. The duo found creative ways to mix graffiti and graphic design. A couple years later, they invaded the web like vandals by conveying their personal style through digital media. In 2007, they opened a studio in Montréal, specializing in branding and logo creation, character design, art direction, and graffiti. At the same time, 123KLAN launched their in-house brand BANDIT-1$M. This hyper-active couple tours the world to share their talent through lectures, murals, and shows. They currently live and work in Montreal, Canada.

P028-031

Akvilė Magicdust

www.akvilemagicdust.com

Akvilė Magicdust is an illustrator based in Vilnius, Lithuania, who enjoys creating surreal, naive, dreamy, poetic stories, comics as well as acrylic paintings.

P042-043

Alejandro Giraldo

www.alejogiraldo.com

Alejandro Giraldo is an illustrator from Medellín, Colombia. Currently, he spends his time working on freelance projects for different clients around the world but also takes time to express himself by working on personal projects, which include illustration, lettering, and fashion. When he is not drawing he is probably thinking about what to eat or what to draw next. He loves the ocean and one day he hopes to live by the sea.

P040-041

Alexander Shimanov

www.behance.net/shimanov

Alexander Shimanov is a Russian graphic designer and old school graffiti writer based in Nizhny Novgorod. He concentrates on streetwear design and corporate identity in retro style for business with soul.

P068-069

Ana Costov

www.anacostov.com

Ana Costov is an artist, illustrator, and dreamer. What inspires and keeps her creating is the desire of the soul to wander through the whole world, experience nature, and connect to the supreme Creator. When this need cannot be fulfilled, she re-creates worlds and places with faces that she has seen or she will never see. She mixes traditional tools like pencils, liners, watercolors, and acrylics with digital techniques like Photoshop and Illustrator. The main point in her work is to express herself and make the viewer feel something.

P214-215

Andrés Yeah

andresyeah.com

Born in Rosario, Argentina in 1987, Andrés Yeah is a graphic designer, illustrator, and art director. After working for some agencies in several cities like Rosario, Buenos Aires, and New York, he now works as a freelance designer on projects related to music, fashion, culture, arts, and human and animal rights.

P044-045

Anton Abo

orkacollective.com

Anton Abo is a graphic designer and illustrator based in Kyiv, Ukraine. He is a member of Orda Collective, and the art director and co-owner of the Ukrainian clothing brand Syndicate Original.

P170-171

Bene Rohlmann

www.benerohlmann.de

Bene Rohlmann is an illustrator and artist based in Berlin, Germany. His illustrations have been published in magazines, newspapers, books, and on album covers, T-shirts, and toys. His art has been shown in many exhibitions worldwide. He mainly works on drawing and collage, but he is always curious to experiment with new techniques.

P124-127

his birthplace, Messina in Sicily, to follow his dream of drawing. He has enjoyed drawing since childhood. He just follows the line, letting the objects take shape and connect in unexpected ways. He likes black ink, black and white color schemes, strong primary colors, and cleanness.

Gabriel Holzner

www.createdbygabe.com

Gabriel Holzner, a.k.a. Gabe, is an illustrator and designer based in Munich, Germany. Whilst working on projects for a broad range of clients, such as Adidas, Reebok, Google, Fred Perry, The Quiet Life, Ray Ban, and so on, Gabe still produces lots of personal works. His love for graphic design, illustration, and life finds manifestation in his own label. He creates apparel of all kinds, prints, and artworks.

Gabe's work was exhibited in Los Angeles, New York, London, and Munich.

Giorgia Lancellotti

www.giorgialancellotti.com

Giorgia Lancellotti is a graphic designer and illustrator based in Italy. She works for brands on apparel design, editorial design, advertising, and for anyone who has a fun project.

Helen Borg

www.behance.net/Miss_Borg

Helen Borg studied graphic design at Durban University of Technology in South Africa. She has developed a style out of doodling candid visuals which is cheeky and inspiring. She always aspires to appeal to the audience with a sense of humor.

Igor Khrupin

www.behance.net/eezo

Igor Khrupin is a designer specializing in business communication services, mainly logo design, brand identity, restaurant branding, rebranding, corporate and brand guidelines, packaging, illustration, and typography.

Isabella Ahmadzadeh

www.behance.net/imzd

Isabella Ahmadzadeh is an art director and illustrator working in Florence, Italy. Since her adolescence, she has always wanted to convey the beauty of things and life through her drawings and visual inspirations. She is currently working as a graphic designer at Gucci.

Isoì

isoi.co

Founded by Gaia Bernasconi, an illustrator, and Daniele Desperati, a graphic designer, Isoì is an indepent creative agency adept at clothing and craft design. They create original and artistic illustrations and handicraft using various techniques like screen printing, engraving, printing press, gold leaf, and so on. Usually they draw inspiration from many things such as landscapes of Ionia in Greece or iconographical art.

Jagoda Jankowska

www.behance.net/jagodajankowska

Jagoda Jankowska is a student majoring in Graphic Design from Poland. After finishing her study in local art school, she has engaged herself in different areas of graphic design such as logo, illustration, branding, visual communication, and pattern design. In each field, she always tries to tell a little story.

Jairo Díaz Herrera

www.behance.net/JairoDiazH

Jairo Díaz is a designer and illustrator from Palmira, Colombia. He has participated as one of the finalists for Behance Portfolio Review 2015 in the category of illustration. He is also the winner of Visual Attack Cali Colombia 2016, and his work is published in the Chilean magazine TRAUMA.

Jakub Rafael

www.behance.net/actiondaycrew

Jakub Rafael is an illustrator and graphic designer from the Czech Republic, who loves hand-drawn illustrations in combination with digital coloring. Aside from design, he also does music and lyrics writing for the music label TY NIKDY under the pseudonym MC GEY.

Juan Díaz-Faes

juandiazfaes.com

Based in Madrid, Juan Díaz-Faes once worked as a camera operator and cartoonist. He started working as an illustrator in 2011. He has obtained his Bachelor of Fine Arts in 2005 and then a Doctorate on the Creative Process. His work tends to have a great graphic and narrative weight. He collaborates monthly with several magazines such as MUWOM and Yorokobu. He is part of the collective Ultrarradio, where new artists publish their work and spread the culture of drawing, comic book events, workshops, publications, and exhibitions. He is also a professor of the One Year Course in Illustration at IED Visual Madrid.

Keiji Ishida

www.behance.net/IshidaKeiji

As an artist, Keiji Ishida enjoys using textures and bright colors in memory of his childhood. However, he also contrasts this innocent world with some obscure symbols from reality, such as a political message or social affair, to express his feelings of being caught in these two worlds. Though Keiji is an independent artist, he takes opportunities to collaborate with other artists to enhance his creativity and explore new styles.

P190

Kevin Bongang

www.bongang.com

Kevin Bongang is a man of many talents and few words. Born in Cameroon, West Africa and raised in Savannah, Georgia in the USA, Kevin Bongang majored in illustration at Atlanta College of Art, where he was able to hone his signature style awash in bold colors, swirling lines, and out-there imagery with a result that is cohesive and truly unique. He has collaborated with the likes of Bucketfeet footwear, Hodgepodge Coffee House & Gallery, Mailchimp, and so on.

P186-187

Leanna Perry

www.leannaperry.com

Leanna Perry is a designer and artist based in Brooklyn, New York. Drenched in intricate hand-drawn patterns and bold graphics, her work is infused with a lust for urban exploring, street fashion, sweaty nightclubs, abandoned buildings, luxury textiles, deep house, and black metal. Leanna's recent clients include Adidas, MAC Cosmetics, Forever 21, GAP, *i-D Magazine*, Target, Urban Outfitters, *Tidal Magazine,* and so on.

P232

Lei Melendres

www.behance.net/leimelendres

Lei Melendres is an illustrator and professional doodle artist whose works have been featured in different esteemed publications, art and design websites, as well as local and international galleries and exhibitions. Lei provides a general mix of

creativity by using what he calls "Infinity Mix," his peculiar style, which describes the intensity of endless details and elements that interact together to form a scene. His doodle art is defined by repetition, patterns, monsters, animals, unimaginable creatures, the unknown, and other weird stuff.

P172-175

Luiso Mostacho

www.blackmouthco.com

Luiso Mostacho is a freelance illustrator and creative director born in Gran Canaria, Spain, who currently settles in London. Being a self-taught artist with a creative mind, Luiso is a passionate devotee of old-school style who enjoys working directly with ink on paper. He is well known for his monochromatic palette with a range of neat illustrations. He has created BlackMouth Co. in 2014, and ever since this brand has evolved into something more than just new media for illustrations. It also represents a raw reality of personal perception of the world.

P070-071, 136

Marcos Navarro

www.marcosnavarro.es

Marcos Navarrol is an illustrator based in Basque Country from Barcelona, Spain. He has developed his professional career throughout the fields of painting, fashion, and street art. His work has been influenced by nature, as well as by urban subcultures. Currently he develops illustrations for music, press, and fashion industry.

P164-165

Mario Carpe

www.behance.net/jagodajankowska

Mario Carpe is an award-winning Spanish creative, fresh, funky and wacky designer and illustrator based in Prague, Czech Republic. He was born in Cadiz, the south of Spain, in 1986 with a pencil in hand. He has

worked in the fields of advertising, branding, print and web design, publishing, and fashion. His works have been awarded and exhibited in cities such as Madrid and Barcelona.

P188-189

Maxim Ignat'ev

www.behance.net/ignatevmaxim

Maxim Ignat'ev, a.k.a. IGNAT'EV INK, is an Illustrator, tattoo artist, and painter from St. Petersburg, Russia.

P104, 122, 156-158

Michael Hacker

www.michaelhacker.at

Michael Hacker is an illustrator and comic artist from Austria. Since 2007 he has been designing and printing live show posters for bands like Queens of the Stone Age, Green Day, Kvelertak, Mastodon, The Melvins, and Red Fang. His clients include Penguin Books, Red Bull, Greenpeace, Slash Snowboards, and magazines like *Vice*, *Kerrang!*, or *GEOlino*. He recently finished his second comic book *Steroid Max* — a homage to 80's and 90's action films.

P110-111, 208

Mighty Harbour Studio

www.behance.net/iqbalhakimboo

Co-founded by Iqbal Hakim Boo, Mighty Harbour Studio is a design agency based in Kuala Lumpur, Malaysia, specializing in graphic design, illustration, branding consultation, and product merchandise. Their works are well inspired by street art and lifestyle.

P088-091, 114-117

Mighty SHORT

mightyshort.com

Originally from France, Mighty SHORT, a.k.a. Davy Le Chevance, is a French graphic artist specialized in branding, apparel design, and

illustration. In 2010 he started as a freelancer in the West Coast of France before he moved to the USA in 2014. His portfolio includes collaborations with famous clients like Nike, Coca-Cola, Adidas Neo, ESPN, Hasbro, Mattel, Neff, Tony Hawk, Element Skateboards, DeLaSoul, and WWE, etc.

Monika Yaneva

www.monikayaneva.com

Monika Yaneva is a Bulgarian designer and illustrator based in London. She graduated from the University of Westminster with a BA Degree(Hons) in Illustration and Visual Communication. Her work is an exciting mixture between color and humor. Monika's work has been exhibited in various venues around London, including Tate Modern. As a graphic designer she creates work mainly for the restaurant and food industries. She spends her time exploring and being fascinated. The rest of the time she draws.

Mr. Kone

wwww.mrkone.com.mx

Mr. Kone is an art director and illustrator based in Mexico. He works for a multitude of magazines and clients globally such as Group PepsiCo, Lipton Mexico, Lipton Europe, MTV, Coca-Cola International, Sony-BMG, Universal Music, Adidas, Mini Cooper, Nike Mexico, Nike USA, and some other brands. He has given numerous lectures and workshops at different events. His work has been published in several national and international books.

Mr Woody Woods

mrwoodywoods.myportfolio.com

Manchester based illustrator, Mr Woody Woods is a ginger bearded obsessive doodler. His bright and bold illustrations have gained a group of loyal followers who love his oddball sense of humor and his ever-growing family of characters. Woody started his illustration career by creating the epic blog project Woody Rather, a series of over 500 illustrated conundrums based on the popular pub game *Would You Rather*, which attracted a lot of attention. His followers continue to be entertained as his work develops across different mediums.

Natalia Pastukhova, Alexey Ponomarchuk

www.behance.net/hellopepe
www.behance.net/alexeyponomarchuk

Natalia Pastukhova and Alexey Ponomarchuk are designers based in Russia.

Natalia Zerko

nataliazerko.com

Natalia Zerko is a freelance graphic designer and illustrator based in Poznan, Poland. Currently she is working closely with Kommunikat design studio on various branding projects.

Olesya Bogoley

www.behance.net/ols_dsgn

After graduation from the local art college, the Russian-based designer Olesya Bogoley began working for some studios specializing in typography, graphic design, and advertisement. It was a good experience for her as she was always obsessed with visual arts. In her works, she tries to show the stylish graphics with interesting themes and to express another world view. Her inspiration draws from art, music, and street culture.

Oscar Fernández

www.behance.net/osc_art

Oscar Fernández is a designer living and working in Buenos Aires, Argentina. For the past few years, he has been involved in multiple projects ranging from animation digital design to branding and graphic design. His work is focused on the quality of things. He pays special attention to the details in order to communicate a clear and precise message.

Pamela Gallegos

www.pomgraphicdesign.com

Pamela Gallegos, a Peruvian Artist born in Miami, is the vision behind Pom Graphic Design. Living in a country with such a rich culture is where her story begins. She makes a connection between nature and the art within it, which is manifested in her designs. Her art focuses on natural elements in all their force. Viewers can see many organic and geometrical multicolor shapes in each piece. The fabulous colors, textures, and shapes that she uses speak about a wonderful world — a world in which cultures and dreams mix together.

Pamela Potgieter

www.behance.net/pamelapotgieter

Pamela Potgieter is a BA graduate on Visual Communication from Stellenbosch Academy of Design and Photography. She majored in illustration. Currently she works predominantly on collage and line drawing. Most of her illustrations are done by hand. Pamela came from a family with a keen interest in the outdoors, and grew up by the ocean, thus her work is greatly influenced by people, nature, and surf and skate culture. Overall her illustrations are also a reflection of her sense of humor.

Petr Kudláček

lilkudley.cz

Petr Kudláček is a graphic designer, art director, and occasional illustrator from Prague, Czech Republic. He acquired his work experience during the four years when he worked in a multidisciplinary studio called Fundaluka. Since 2013 he has been freelancing under the name Lilkudley. He enjoys engaging himself in visual identity design greatly, ranging from creating website design to selecting colored paper for business cards. In order to make these projects possible, he stays in touch and collaborates with competent programmers, motion designers, and photographers.

P152–153

Raül Garcia Gili

www.raulgarciagili.com

Raül Garcia Gili is an interdisciplinary designer based in Spain. He adores simple and meaningful things. He reads, explores, and discovers his own little world, trying to find new ideas in little things that would make the viewer think and feel.

P185

Riccardo Sabatini

www.behance.net/riccardosabatini

Riccardo Sabatini is a hobby artist and graphic designer from Italy. His works have been seen in some books, art exhibitions, and online publications.

P092–099

Rubens Scarelli

www.rubensscarelli.com

Rubens Scarelli, a.k.a. Rusc, is a freelance illustrator from the southeast of Brazil.

P100–103

Sam Dunn

www.sam-dunn.com

Sam Dunn is an freelance illustrator based in East London. She grew up in Hartlepool, a fading seaside town in the far northeast of England, and spent her weekends exploring the dense forests of the Lake District National Park. Her work is delicately crafted by hand with pen and ink and colored digitally with many layers of textures, which aims to preserve the warm and tangible appearance of traditional media.

P022–027

Sebastian Mueller

www.behance.net/endor
www.darkerhalfcult.com
www.blackclouddesign.com

Born in the 1980s, Sebastian Mueller is a graphic designer and illustrator from Cologne, Germany. He is the owner of the Endor Design and co-founder of the Darker Half Cult. His work is focused on art direction, brand identity, graphic design, illustration. In 2015, he teamed up with Chris Weiss (owner of the Black Cloud Design) and founded the Darker Half Cult, to express their love for underground music and urban culture, and their strong will to make a lasting impact on the local design of Cologne. His clients include bands and brands like Universal Music, Bravado Merchandise, Fearless Records, Volbeat, Bad Religion, Heaven Shall Burn, and so on.

P074–083

Simón Londoño Sierra

www.behance.com/lemonsta

Simón Londoño, a.k.a. Le Monsta, is a lettering artist, creative director, and illustrator who aspires to make well-crafted images for brands and projects. Typography and illustration work together within his work, which mix together until one hardly knows where the type or illustration starts. This Colombian artist uses illustration and letter design as a way to communicate and turns them into a language with more strength and style.

P036–037, 058–059

Sofia Noceti

sofianoceti.com

From branding to graphic design, art direction, and publishing, Sofia Noceti, a designer and illustrator from Buenos Aires, continuously embeds her multidisciplinary talent into her creations, which is always infused with her instantly recognizable aesthetic, detailing ethereal compositions, and whimsical color palettes.

P200–201

The Feebles

www.thefeebles.com

After collaborating with one another for 10 years, Gaëtan Guerlais and Anaël Moreau finally founded their own studio the Feebles in 2013. They are adept at graphic design and illustration. Driven by the spirit of freedom and curiosity, their work is often bold and intelligent, mixing different techniques and tools. They create a world that is fun and modern, yet they value efficiency and believe that the image is to convey the message. There is a tacit mutual understanding between the duo, which enables them to work on each project together and conceive a common vision. The Feebles, it is about a story of encounters, reflections, creations, ideas, tools, laughter, embraces, design, and happiness.

P216–217

The Red Wolf

www.theredwolf.pt

The Red Wolf is a Portuguese brand of illustration and design. The brand is a joint venture, created by Filipe Duarte and Joana Campos Silva in 2016, who both work from their home studio based in Oporto, Portugal. Filipe Duarte has worked as a designer since 2001 in the areas of graphic design and multimedia. Joana Campos Silva is a fashion specialist in strategy and brand development, creative projects management, and networking.

Tianlin Ma

www.behance.net/felix_shaozi

Tianlin Ma is a designer and illustrator from China.

Tikkywow

www.behance.net/tikkywow

Tikkywow, a.k.a. Pichet Rujivararat, is a Thai artist living in Bangkok, Thailand. He often collaborates with many Thai and international artists, and works with some famous brands like Nike, G-Shock watch, Line, Playing Arts, Tiger Beer, Thai Airways, Camel, Bangkok Auto Salon, etc. His work ranges from logo, graphic design, product design, and special event. Designed with love and passion, he hopes that his work brings happiness to the viewer.

Tony Riff

www.tonyriff.com

Tony Riff is a London based graphic designer and illustrator. His style stands out with colors and unexpected figures which are eye-catching and fun.

Valístika Studio

www.valistika.com

Formed in 2006, Valístika is a visual studio based in Madrid, focusing on illustration, typography, branding, and graphics applied to clothing, advertising, editorial, and all fields related to print and motion media. They work with clients all over the globe.

Venya Son

www.behance.net/sonbalon

Venya Son is a young artist from Kiev, Ukraine who currently works in Barcelona, Spain. He graduated from National Technical University of Ukraine Kiev Polytechnic Institute with a Degree in Illustration. Meanwhile, he has supervised a few exhibitions with the collaboration of Ukrainian streetwear brands and other artists. Venya creates digital arts as well as traditional ones with watercolors and acrylic on canvas. His works are very colorful and usually highlight social issues.

Verónica de Arriba

www.depeapa.com

Verónica de Arriba, a.k.a Depeapa, is an illustrator and designer based in Spain. After studying Fine Arts in Basque Country located in the north of Spain, Verónica worked as a graphic designer in Granada for several years, but in 2007 she felt the urge to draw again. Then in 2008, she founded Depeapa, a home goods and accessories brand based in Granada, Spain. "Depeapa" originates from the Spanish expression "de pe a pa," which means "from A to Z."

Volga Ilyina

www.behance.net/VolgaIlyina

Volga Ilyina is a designer from Minsk, Belarus. She has loved drawing since her childhood. She draws everywhere and on everything, from wallpaper to cupboards, sand, garments, and paper. She went to the art school in her native city Mogilev, and then moved on to Belarusian State Academy of Arts in Minsk. After finishing her studies, she started to work as a designer. She loves to find art in simple things no matter if the inspiration comes from nature, urban landscapes, or classical art.

Why Duck

www.why-duck.com

Why Duck, a.k.a Krystian Ścigalski, is an illustrator from Poland. He conceives, figures, and imagines before seizing a brush. His work smells of pencil, ink, and marker pens.

ACKNOWLEDGEMENTS

We would like to thank all of the designers involved for granting us permission to publish their works, as well as all of the photographers who have generously allowed us to use their images. We are also very grateful to many other people whose names do not appear in the credits but who made specific contributions and provided support. Without these people, we would not have been able to share these beautiful works with readers around the world. Our editorial team includes editor Jessie Tan and book designer Dingding Huo, to whom we are truly grateful.